AGAINST
ALL ODDS

From the Projects to the Penthouse

Mahisha Dellinger

BROWN GIRLS BOOKS

Houston, Texas * Washington, D.C.

Against All Odds © 2015 by Mahisha Dellinger
Brown Girls Publishing, LLC
www.browngirlspublishing.com
ISBN: 9781625177063 (eISBN)
  9781625177070 (print ISBN)

First Brown Girls Publishing LLC trade printing

Manufactured and Printed in the United States of America

Table of Contents

A Note From The Author...

I cannot attempt to thank anyone before I give my upmost thanks to my Almighty Father. Thank you Lord for all that you have done for me. Without Your grace, mercy and provision I wouldn't be who and where I am today. Thank You for Your covering, every day.

To my husband, my lover, my partner and my best friend. Our journey together is nothing short of miraculous. Thank you for always supporting my journey, even when it means less time with you. You selfishly give to me, daily. Thank you for being the amazing father you are to our beautiful children. I love you.

To my mother, thank you for always having my back and being in my corner when no one else is. Thank you for always believing in me. You always have been, and always will be my biggest cheerleader, and for that, I thank you. Your love and support has enabled me to become who I am today and your undying faith in God has created the foundation for my family and me. For this, I am eternally grateful.

To my father, David Vernon, I wish you were here to see me now! You were always so proud of me…your opinion has always meant so much to me. You were my hero, the epitome of an amazing man. Your life was cut short; I am living my life for your memory and honor. You set the example for me of how education can change your life. Your example lit my path.

To my grandparents, Dave and Ola Vernon, thank you for giving me the one and only example of a successful martial union. "Till death do us part", you vowed and you did. Being in your home, every weekend, gave me refugee, unconditional love and hope that I could also have a happy marriage. Grandma Ola, there isn't a day that goes by that I don't miss and long for you. I miss you so much. I love you more than words can express. You passed away over 20 years ago yet the pain feels like day one. If I could only see you one more time.

To my beautiful children Kiana, Bryce, Isabella, and Kennedy. Thank you for being my muses. Everything I do is for you.

Kiana...my firstborn child, the reason why I worked so hard to change my destiny, our destiny. You were so precious to me that I vowed to give you the best life I could. I thank you for unapologetically being you: smart, beautiful, special and set apart by God. Continue to make your mark, unafraid of how others will perceive you. What God has for you, no man can take away.

Bryce...my handsome little man, my one and only son. You are such a brilliant soul destined for GREAT things. I am so proud of who you are. Your gentle spirit will move mountains. You are sincerely kind, special and hand picked by God. I am proud to be your mother.

Isabella...you were destined to be here. From the moment you were born, your fire and determination was evident. I love how independent and confident you are. You are like me in so many ways. I love who you are becoming and where you are going. World watch out!

Kennedy...my baby, God blessed me with you. I dreamed of you. Thank you for loving me the way you do. You turn all of my bad days into good days. I know that no matter happens, you are there to tell me how much you love me. Your spirit is old, kind, and a God send.

Katrina, my sister...not by birth, but by spirit. We have been through so much together. I know I can always count on you to be open, honest and supportive of me. Thank you for being in my corner, though every stage of my life.

Marla, my calm through every storm, when I couldn't talk to my husband, I reached out for you. When I feel that life is too much, you remind me of how much God has blessed me and my family. Thank you for being in my corner.

To my publisher, Brown Girl Books, thank you for taking a chance on me. Your trust, and faith in me means the world to me.

To my Publicist, Tyrah Lindsey. I admire you for so many reasons. You were able to penetrate professional barriers left foreign to me. You are the quintessential example of true success.

To my CURLS team, Monica King, Victor Armendarez, Tiffany Torres, Viet Trinh, Yumi Nguyen…you are my core: those that I count on when things get tough. You all have been an instrumental part of the CURLS legacy. I appreciate you.

To Target Corporation, specifically Linda Sullivan. Thank you for taking a chance with CURLS. Your faith in my brand propelled my business forward, and for that, I am eternally grateful. You will always have a special place in my heart.

To my vendors that continue to support me by stocking my products on your shelf. Thank you for taking a chance on a young brand.

To my CURLS customers, thank you for your continued support, dedication, and love of the brand. Without you, none of this would be possible.

To all of my friends, family and favorite cousins (you know who you are) that shared this journey with me. Thank you for the good, bad, fun and sad times we shared. Each experience shared helped to shape me into the woman I have become today.

INTRODUCTION

I've always known I was destined for great things. Don't ask me how I knew. I just did. It definitely couldn't have been my environment. After all, the mean streets of Sacramento can shatter anyone's dreams. In fact, my Meadowview neighborhood was dubbed "Danger Island" and although it was nestled between the affluent Pocket/Green haven area and lower middle class, Mack Road, it was not a place you wanted to be caught outside after dark.

I definitely didn't have the support at home. It's not that my family didn't believe in me and want more, but my mother was working so hard—and so long—that dreams (hers and mine) took a back seat.

However, I knew that I wouldn't allow someone else to write my story. I knew that my story was bigger than the impoverished streets I called home. And now, as my company, CURLS LLC, boasts its best year to date, I look back and reflect on where I've been and where I'm going.

I'm hoping that my story will inspire others to take their own journeys, to not let their pasts dictate their future, to go for their dreams and not let anything or anyone get in their way. While my story may be deemed a rags to riches tale, it's bigger than that. So much bigger. It's about an ordinary girl who decided she was capable of extraordinary things. It's about a woman who took all the obstacles tossed in her path of life and used them as stepping-stones to bigger and better things.

I truly have come from humble beginnings and as I worked my way up through the rigors of corporate America, the ups and downs of being an entrepreneur, the frustrations of trying to maintain a proper work-family balance, I've learned some valuable lessons. They are lessons that I share with you in the coming pages. From the pitfalls to the pinnacles, I bare it all.

Now, as my company—which started from my kitchen—is poised to post-record sales, I'm sharing my journey. Not only of how I overcame an impoverished background to pursue my passion, but also of how I went from just dreaming to *doing*. With valuable, applicable tips, it is my hope that after reading, the entrepreneurial spirit within you will be awakened.

My story can be your story. And if you walk away with nothing else, I hope that you'll understand my motto: When you wake up in the morning you have two choices—go back to sleep and dream your dreams, or wake up and chase your dreams.

I choose the latter. What will your choice be?

— *Mahisha*

1
A Tale of Two Worlds

I'm not supposed to be here.

At least that's what the statistics said. According to all the studies, and the declarations of negative people in my life, if I did survive my gang-riddled neighborhood, it would be unwed with several children by my side, a dead-end, low-paying job, and a future that lacked hope. That's what the statistics said.

But I had a different ending for my story.

I never have settled for the norm. Even as a little girl, from a broken home, I knew that my destiny was greater than my existence. After all, I'd survived abuse, and my life had been spared more times than I could count.

Given my background, I could've easily become that sassy, tell-you-off, around-the-way girl who ran with the dope boys and held her own in the streets. Quite the contrary, though, I was about as close to perfection as you could get in a child.

With flopping pigtails and a smile that melted everyone I met, people in the neighborhood knew that I wasn't like the rest of the girls. From a very young age, I was a very self-motivated, independent, and simply, an easy child to raise. I never got in trouble (I would occasionally mouth off, but my mother was quick to pop me in my mouth to get me back in line). I was where I was supposed to be, when I was supposed to be there.

However, one day, I wasn't where I was supposed to be—at John Sloat Elementary School. To this day, I believe my mother's boyfriend, Willie, is to blame.

My daily routine was the same—my mom left for work

at 7 a.m. I got myself up, dressed, and off to school by 8:30 a.m. Willie was always the last person to leave before me, he knew that the garage was my only way out. I didn't have a house key (my brother did because he always made it home from school before me, so I didn't need one). Willie knew that I exited through the kitchen into the garage, manually lifting the exterior garage door. This day was like no other, except when I went to lift the wooden garage door to head to school, it was locked. I had already locked the door to the house so I couldn't get out. I was stuck!

I knew I would miss school that day. I hated missing school. I hated getting behind. Still, I didn't panic, at first, even though I was afraid. I tried to pick the lock—no luck. I was eight years old and had no idea what I was doing. I tried to kick in the door. Nothing. I weighed all of sixty pounds so I don't know what I thought I was doing anyway. After accepting that I wasn't going anywhere, I had to find a way to keep busy, for nearly nine hours. I sorted and folded the clothes in the dryer. I swept the entire garage, organized every item I could get my hands on. When I finished that I discovered that only an hour had passed!

I reviewed my spelling words again, I checked my homework again, and I read another chapter in my history book. After three hours I started to panic. I was really scared and started to weep. My cries were interrupted by a voice.

"Hello, is there someone in there?"

It was the mailman!

"Yes! I'm locked in!" I screamed.

"What is your name?" he asked through the garage door.

"Mahisha. Mahisha Vernon," I anxiously replied. "Help me, please. I'm stuck in here."

"Who can I call for you?" he asked.

"Please call my mom," I said, giving him my work number.

"Okay, I'll be right back."

I would later learn that he went to my neighbor's house and called my mother. She was frantic but she couldn't leave her job, so she called my uncle, Calvin, who lived close by. As long as I can remember, my Uncle Calvin always came to our rescue. When my mother's car was stolen, for the third and final time, a week before Christmas, he gave her a car to use for two years until she could get another one. He has always had a kind, giving spirit and that day was no exception. Uncle

Calvin came to my rescue ten minutes later! He cut the lock off of the garage door, even cutting up his hand pretty badly. I don't think I'd ever been so happy to see someone! And I was even happier to be out of that garage. Uncle Calvin gave me a big hug and took me for a ride on his motorcycle. My mom was upset with Willie that day, even though he swore he didn't purposely lock the garage. I didn't believe him, but we could never prove otherwise.

As much as I wanted to go off, I let the incident go. That was my nature. I was far from a troublemaker. There were never any surprises me with so there was never any need to ground or punish me.

Yes, my mother was able to relax with me. It was, however, a totally different story for my brother. He was more than a handful and caused my mother enough grief for the both of us.

My parents never married. They were from two different worlds and the worlds could never seem to mesh. While his family lived a life of privilege, my mother's family lived a life of poverty. So for her, and subsequently us, every day was a struggle. In those days, women didn't file for child support and so the burden of caring for me and my brother fell solely on my mother. Don't get me wrong, my dad took care of my living expenses, but my day-to-day existence was meager.

Every day I saw a tale of two worlds, from the impoverished school I attended, to the graffiti laden streets that I walked, I saw the worst that Sacramento had to offer. But just as soon as I settled into that life, I would be whisked away to spend weekends in the suburbs with my father. There, I would experience the best that life had to offer. Visits to museums, exotic restaurants, and cultural landmarks one day. Drive-bys, gang wars, and home invasions the next.

But my primary world was with my mother, where I fell asleep to the sound of gunfire, where it was nothing for a gang to come kick in your front door. In fact, I saw the gang life up close and personal as my brother was a member of the Meadowview Blood's, a notorious street gang.

As vastly different as the two worlds were, each played a role in the woman that I've become. As a little girl, those two worlds became the sum of my existence.

My parent's backgrounds were so different. My dad's family put an emphasis on education, all of their descendants ended up doing something amazing with their lives. My dad was an engineer and almost everyone in his family was educated. Eric Holder, who served as US Attorney General twice, married a cousin on my dad's side, Sharon Malone, who is an obstetrician and gynecologist. If you Google another relative, Vivian Malone, you'll see she did so many amazing things in history. She was the first black woman to graduate from the University of Alabama, amongst many other amazing accomplishments. Jeff Malone is a retired NBA star. Most of our relatives have completed college and all are doing well in life.

So maybe that drive to succeed is ingrained within me. All I know is for all that I did inherit from my father's side; I inherited just as much from my mother's side.

Living in the hood gave me the strength, endurance, perseverance, determination, and sheer will to fight. I am one tough cookie. Don't be fooled by my Chanel bag and Louboutin heels.

Sure, my mom's side of the family was the total opposite.

My grandmother, the daughter of a slave, lived in the hood, had nine children, and adopted the tenth. Her mother raised her first two children. She was married and left by a host of husbands. Given all of her trials and tribulation, she led by example. She was a praying woman with faith so strong she didn't worry about where their next meal was going to come from.

Because of the time I spent with my dad, I started to feel like I didn't belong in the hood. My dad dressed me, he bought me expensive clothes that I wore in the hood with kids who wore the same clothes every day. I had the same amount of money they had—I was poor. I never felt like I belonged anywhere. I was an oddity.

So, while he was showering me with my material needs, my mother made sure all of my emotional needs were met.

I learned about the finer things in life with my dad. How I deserved nice things, how education and financial security could lay the foundation for a successful future.

From my mother, I learned the essence of hard work. As long as I can remember, my mom never was without a job.

But that working took its toll on us. Mom was always gone early in the morning, so I remember from second grade on, I would get myself up on time, comb my hair, get myself dressed, prepare my breakfast, pack my snack and walk to school.

"There goes little Miss Vernon," my neighbor would say as I traipsed down the street. "Always on point."

I'd wave, never breaking my stride. I took pride in everyone knowing how I was always so responsible.

We moved every couple of years, so I changed schools a lot and had to learn to make friends fast, adapt quickly and be outgoing. I spent second grade in one school, third grade in another school and so on and so forth each year.

While my schooling may not have been consistent, there was one thing that was constant. Church.

I spent a lot of time at church when I was growing up. My mom gave her life back to God when I was in the sixth grade. Our lives changed forever when we joined Zion Church in Jesus Christ, a strict Apostolic church that didn't allow women to wear pants, make up, or jewelry.

As much as I appreciated all I was getting from church, there was a time when I felt embarrassed because it got to the point that I was teased incessantly, for being the "weird church girl that only wore dresses." Add to that fact that I was in the seventh grade, flat-chested and shy, and it made for a miserable existence.

But little did I know, puberty was about to change my life.

2
Project Girl

My brother was four years older and was supposed to watch me and he did well until his teen years. That's when he started straying away and hanging out in the streets, and the streets became his home. He was always in and out of juvenile facilities for one reason or another, mostly for selling drugs. When he turned eighteen, juvie was upgraded to jail.

On one of his times out, he began selling drugs for a

well-known dealer. The dealer, "Jimmy," had several of the young boys on the corner selling drugs for him.

The young boys selling crack would get caught and get sent to jail while Jimmy made a profit. I remember many days, my mom would go to Jimmy's house and pull my brother out and bring him home and he'd turn around and go right back the next day. She was so stressed out about my brother because there was always something going on with him. And that something usually ended up hurting us.

At one point, my brother's childhood friends and fellow gang members, (brothers, JJ and Junior Smith) were in the midst of a battle with rival gang members. The gang members raided JJ and Junior's home looking for them. They weren't home, but their mother, Patty, was. As it goes with gang members, they knew the way to hurt JJ and Junior the most would be to hurt those that they loved.

Patty took a fatal gunshot to the chest.

Of course, the brothers were devastated, as was their little sister, Tanisha, who I was friends with. Since our brothers did their dirt together, I remember thinking, "That could have been my mother."

The violence did hit our home—literally—when I was fifteen.

I remember that day I knew that my life would be different. That there was a purpose to my existence. At fifteen, my paternal grandparents had given me a car. This was major for a kid growing up in the hood. There were grown folks in my neighborhood that didn't have cars.

I was too young to drive the Nissan Datsun so my mother made sure it stayed parked. One day, I wanted to take the car and go hang out with my best friend, more like sister, Katrina. I begged my mother to let us use the car.

"Mom, please, I really want to drive the car," I pleaded.

My mother had tried her best to raise me and my brother, but as a single mother there was only so much she could do. She didn't like giving in to me, but I knew she was feeling some guilt because she'd been working so much lately.

She hesitated, then said, "Mahisha, you know you're too young to drive."

"Please, Katrina has her license….she can drive!" I begged, even though I knew the chances were slim.

Finally, my mother inhaled deeply and said, "Fine."

I sat stunned for a minute because I really hadn't expected her to say yes. But I jumped up and threw my arms around her neck. "Thank you mom!"

Katrina and I left without a care in the world. And then, not fifteen minutes after we left, tragedy struck.

My mother would later tell me that we had just pulled off when the sound of gunfire lit up the night and our living room. Gunmen had unleashed a hail of bullets into the whole front side of our house. Bedrooms, the living room, all riddled with bullets. But what made my heart drop, was the bullet we found lodged in "my chair." The chair I always sat in, engaged in many "deep" conversations with Katrina. The chair I was sitting in right before my mother went against her usual judgment and gave me permission to go out.

My mom felt it was divine intervention that she let us go that night. Maybe I wouldn't have been there at that moment; maybe I would've been in the bathroom or something, but that was the chair where I often sat, and there was a good chance that I would've been sitting in it at the time of the shooting.

That miraculous moment redefined my existence. What happened shortly after that drive-by shooting made me even more determined to live a different live.

It was a sunny June day, shortly after my fifteenth birthday. I was hanging out with one of my favorite cousins, Shelly and her boyfriend, Roger. Roger and one of his friends both had scooters, so we decided to take a joy ride. His friend was just my type— smooth mocha skin, curly hair, nicely dressed. I liked him. He seemed like a nice guy and he was digging me since my flat chest had filled out and I had come into my own as a beautiful young girl. I thought we were a good match. My instincts couldn't have more wrong.

In that moment—zipping through the streets of Sacramento on the back of his scooter, breezing by familiar territory, I was having the time of my life. At one point, my cousin and Roger sped off and left us behind, or perhaps he slowed down to lose them, I don't know.

After all but coming to a stop, he turned to me and said, "Hey, do you mind if I stop by cousin's house for a minute?"

I was a virgin, so I'll admit I was a little naive because I just said, "Sure."

We went inside his cousin's home. I will never forget that light brown, stucco house with dead trees and battered lawn chairs. I waited in the front room while he disappeared. The next thing I knew, he was calling me from the back.

"Hey, Mahisha, you mind coming back here?" he yelled.

It felt a little weird, but I walked back to where he was. I liked him, and honestly didn't mind if we kissed. Sex was never an option. It didn't even cross my mind because I wasn't interested. I didn't know anything about date rape, so that never crossed my mind either.

Once he shut the door, though, he became another person.

"Come here, girl," he said, pulling me toward him.

The sudden movement caught me by surprise and I immediately jerked back.

"Oh, so that's how you wanna play it?" He laughed as he pushed me down on the bed, then pulled out a gun, laid it by my head, and forced my pants down.

"No!" I cried, tugging at my pants.

We went back and forth in that tug-of-war for a while, and when he picked up the gun and pointed it at my head, I stopped fighting. This wasn't how I imagined my first sexual experience would be. There were no flowers, no 'I love you,' no romance. Just a guy taking me against my will. All force, manipulation, pain and disgust.

The more I cried, the more it seemed to turn him on. He ripped me, in more ways than one. In addition to feeling violated, I now had to worry about the possibility of being pregnant at fifteen, like most of the girls I grew up with.

But more than shame and anger, I felt guilt. In my mind, I was getting what I deserved. I had no business being back there with him in the first place. It was dumb of me to think that the most he would want to do was kiss. This was all my fault. So I laid back, stifled my tears, and let him do what he did.

I don't remember much else after that, except he went on with the evening like nothing was wrong.

"Come on, girl. We need to go catch up with Roger and

your cousin," he said, standing and zipping his pants. If he had any remorse, he didn't show it.

I was numb as he directed me back out to his scooter. I was in shock as I climbed on the back of it as he instructed, and waited for him to take me wherever he was going to take me.

About five minutes into our ride, as he hummed a RunDMC song, a tire blew on his scooter so he pulled over.

I don't know why I viewed that as my chance to escape. But when he stopped, I just jumped off and I ran. And ran, until I was too exhausted to run anymore. I don't even think I knew where I was going. I just knew that I needed to get away from him.

Those few hours after are a blur too. All I know is darkness fell and I was still wandering around. My mother is actually the one who found me a little after nine pm. Since I wasn't one to cause trouble, she had been scouring the neighborhood looking for me, in fear that something horrible happened to me. My mom knew where I was and what I was doing at all times but she hadn't heard from me that evening so she knew something was wrong. Once she found me, she took one look at me and she knew.

"Oh, my, God, baby, what happened?" she asked, taking me into her arms. "Are you okay?"

I couldn't even respond as I collapsed in her arms and cried.

She held me, but kept asking, "What happened? What happened?"

I finally confessed everything.

"Oh my god, I'm calling your father," she immediately said. She wasted no time getting him on the phone and of course, he was furious. Both he and my mother wanted to go directly to the police station. But I refused. I mean, adamantly refused. I didn't want to talk about it and I didn't want to keep reliving it over and over. I acted like it never happened and I buried it. Or so I thought. Little did I know, I would be forever impacted by this act of violence. My life would never be the same. I didn't know if I would ever want to go on another date in my life. I couldn't help but wonder would I ever enjoy and experience true intimacy with a man, with my future husband? How would I ever trust anyone again? I became angry and desolate.

Because I initially never dealt with the rape, I never completely healed. The wounds actually manifested themselves in different ways in my relationships with others, and myself. Looking back, staying silent about what happened was the worst thing I could've done.

One of the things that I've come to realize is no matter how many times we try to move on, unprocessed pain leaves a hole.

It took me years to fill that hole. It took me years to get to the point where I knew what happened to me wasn't my fault, no matter what the actions were leading up to the date rape, I had to reach a point when I accepted that there is nothing that justifies rape, nor does anyone ever "deserve it."

Over the years, I've talked with other victims of date rape, and everyone I talk to feels guilty or ashamed in one way or another. Victims of date rape, myself included, must reach a point of knowing that the person that is deserving of the guilt and shame is the person that chose to do the rape. The rape was not about anything you did, it is about the attacker needing control and they alone are responsible for their actions. As a victim—be it of rape, assault, whatever—you have two options, deal with your problems head on or run from them. The problem is when you run, your demons become your shadow and you can never outrun your shadow. Your shadow is always there, there is no changing the past. The shoulda, coulda, wouldas don't go away. But if you are focusing on the things you do have control over (your present, your future), then you'll be able to move forward. It's a lesson it took me a while to get, but I'm grateful that I did.

3

A Love Like This

Before those life-changing events, I really didn't have any major plans for my life. The only thing I did know, was that I *didn't* want a love like my parents.

Even though my mother hadn't finished school, she was a hustler, and always found a way to make things happen. In fact, that attitude landed her a job at Campbell's Soup, which is where my father was doing an internship in the engineering department. They met one summer at Black Family Day in William Land Park.

A strikingly handsome man, with gorgeous curly hair, a killer smile and a sleek wardrobe, David Vernon was a ladies' man. But my mother didn't care. She wanted him badly. And what she wanted, she usually got.

She told her girlfriend that day, "I am going to get that FINE man!"

My mother's obsession with my father is proof that all that is good *to* you isn't good *for* you. My mother made it her business to look on point every day. She would dress in the baddest outfit, which revealed her perfect size six frame. Her hair and makeup was always together. She made sure my father took notice. And take notice he did.

Eventually, my mom snagged her man. They fell in love and began a tumultuous, dysfunctional, abusive relationship. Because for as much as David Vernon loved her, he never stopped loving other women. Even when I was born— conceived at a Jackson Five concert—her love wasn't enough to make him marry her. It wasn't enough to keep him from straying. It wasn't enough for anything.

Cheating became the norm. He did it and she accepted it. There were so many instances, she eventually lost track.

One she does vividly remember though, was when she was pregnant with me.

"He was in college. I went to go visit him in his apartment on 15th Street, he had a girl in his apartment," my mother recalls. "We got into a big fight and I toppled down the stairs."

Thankfully, she wasn't seriously hurt. Of course, her heart was hurt, but not enough to keep her from going back.

My mother would catch my father cheating, he would get mad and hit her, even though he was the one in the wrong.

But yet, she stayed.

I remember one year I went to a free summer camp for inner city kids. My dad picked me up one day and my coach, a light skinned, curly haired, black woman, saw him and introduced herself. She was smitten! They ended up going out on a date and apparently, they took their relationship "to the next level." My dad never called her back, but she would ask me about him every day.

My dad, the quintessential ladies' man, filled up his truck with presents at Christmas time. I remember stopping by all of these different women's houses with gifts for each one of them. None of the gifts were special purchases. They were all bought at once, they were mass purchases. My father didn't even bother with name tags either. No one was special to him, so he didn't bother.

While I don't excuse or condone any of my father's actions, through the years, I began to question my mother's decision to love a man so hard who treated her so poorly.

David Vernon wasn't the only man to physically assault my mother. I later experienced this firsthand when my mother's boyfriend beat her to a pulp, right in front of me.

I was just seven years old the first time I bore witness to the violence. It was something that would continue until my mother got up the strength to love herself more than she loved any man. And while she did move on, heal herself, she never lost her love for David Vernon.

While my father never married my mother, he did marry two other women, who loved him just as fiercely.

Yet, despite all that love, all the ladies that longed for him, my dad died alone. He died of heart failure and it was unexpected. He was in his house for three days before anyone found him, flies filled the window and his carcass, the stench was unbearable. It was absolutely horrible. He had no wife; no one in his life when he died. Both of his wives left him, and he said he wasn't going to marry again and he never did.

So as much as he loved, there was no one there to love him in his final days.

Because of the way my father's relationships ended, his exes really weren't a factor in the aftermath of his death.

I really loved his first wife, and she loved me. They divorced when my sister was nine months and I still keep in touch with her to this day.

My father's second wife never liked me, so when they divorced there was no love lost as far as I was concerned. Once my dad's second wife left him, he changed his will. He decided that he wanted my sister and I to get all of his money, and he didn't want his ex-wives getting anything so he signed his sister as his beneficiary with strict instructions for her to divide the money between my sister and me.

The whole family knew that was the agreement, but when my father died and my aunt found out how much money he left behind, she decided to keep it for herself. She didn't give us one penny. Because there were never any legal documents dictating my father's wishes, there was nothing I could do about it. We didn't speak for several years and our relationship still isn't the same.

4
The Evolution of My Mother

The viscous cycle of loving the wrong man became a constant for my mother. When I was in the seventh grade, she married a man named Phillip, a deacon at our church. He was also a cheater, a liar and an abuser.

Soon after my mother married Phillip, she found out that he was cheating with a new member of the church. She was devastated!

She was rewarded with her commitment by Phillip getting hooked on drugs. During one of his drug-induced rampages, he robbed his own mother. At one point, he even started to steal tithes and offering from the church, and even stole my brother's hidden stash of crack cocaine, which my brother was waiting to sell.

There came a time when my mother had had enough. She told him that he had to go. He did. But before he left, he doled out a few more punches. . . leaving her with unpaid rent and a black eye.

Her previous live-in boyfriend, Willie, wasn't any better. (Yes, the same Willie that locked me in the garage when I was eight.) This sounds really bad, but I didn't like him at the time because he was a janitor. To me, he represented more of the struggling world that I wanted no part of. My sophisticated father would pick me up in a nice car, wearing nice suits. Willie didn't couldn't compare to my dad.

One night, my mom got all dressed up and planned to go out with her best friend, Suzy. She was on her way out the door and Willie grabbed her and stopped her.

"You're not going anywhere," he told her.

She jerked free. "Are you crazy? I'm going out."

"Who you getting all dressed up for?" he shouted. "You got some other dude you trying to go see?"

My mother calmly tried to talk to him. "Willie, you're being ridiculous. I told you I was going out with friends. I won't be out too late."

With that, my mother turned and headed toward the door. Before she made it two steps, Willie grabbed her by the back of the hair and flung her to the floor.

"Get off my mama!" I yelled, jumping on his back. Of course I wasn't successful in getting him to stop as he just flung my little body to the side.

"Noooo!" she cried as he continued hitting her and punching her in the face. After a while he finally left. My mother ended up with bruises and two black eyes. I knew then, this would never be me.

A week later he came back and apologized and she forgave him and let him move back in.

I could never be with a man that would do something like that, with a man that could invoke so much hate. And I hated him. I hated the sight of him! I hated that my mother forgave him and let him back into our lives. My mom may have forgiven, but I didn't. I prayed for the day that she woke up and saw him the way I did…beneath her!

It would take some time, but my mother would finally see Willie through my eyes. The day she decided to leave him was one of the best days of my life!

It was the last day of school, the beginning of the summer of 1983. The school bell rang and I rushed outside, only to find my mom anxiously waiting for me outside my classroom door.

"Mahisha, get your stuff, we have to hurry," she said in a panic.

"Why? Where are we going mom?" I asked.

"Just hurry!" she shouted.

Our car was filled to the brim with personal belongings, my mattress was strapped to the roof, and my brother was in the front seat waiting. I jumped in the car without asking any more questions, then we sped down Candlewood Way.

"I left Willie for good," my mother finally said. "We are going to stay with Anissa and Vernon," she added, referring to my cousins.

I later learned that instead of going to work my mother picked up my Uncle Calvin and headed to U-Haul to rent a moving truck. She had exactly five hours to pack the house. While my uncle and his sons loaded the truck, my mom filled our car with our clothes, key personal belongings, my mattress, which I guess wouldn't fit in the truck, and a few of my favorite toys. We left 1981 Quincy Way once and for all. The house that Willie tainted with his abusive ways would soon become a distant memory.

It only took us twenty minutes to arrive at my cousin Anissa and her husband, Vernon's apartment. Seven people in a two-bedroom apartment wasn't actually ideal, but anything was better than living with Willie. Besides, our family was really close, someone was always in a some sort of bind, and everyone chips in whenever, however they can.

My family knew that my mom had to get away from Willie. She feared for her life, he promised her that if he couldn't have her no one would. She knew he meant every word. Luckily, he had no idea where my cousins lived so she felt safe there.

I became accustomed to making friends, fast. The second day at Anissa's house, I met a new friend named Stacy. I noticed two cocoa-skinned girls with cornrowed/beaded hair playing in the parking lot. They looked my age, so I introduced myself.

"Hi, my name is Mahisha. What is your name?"

The smallest girl replied. "Stacy, and this my sister, Monique. Where are you from?"

"Meadowview. Can I play with your guys? I asked.

"Sure. If you know how to double dutch!" Stacy replied.

Did I ever! We double-dutched every day until the street lights came on. We swam in the community pool. We walked to the neighborhood candy store together. We were becoming the best of friends. Despite the fact that I always invited Stacy into Cousin Anissa's apartment, she never invited me inside hers. They lived upstairs from us. She said her stepfather was really mean and we didn't want to see him angry. I shrugged and let it go.

My mother started to ask me questions about Stacy and her family. As always, mom had a discerning spirit. She knew something wasn't quite right. Stacy never had a curfew. When I was summoned inside, Stacy and Monique were allowed to stay out. My mom instantly took notice.

A few weeks later my mom sat me down and told me she had to tell me something.

"What mom? I want to go and see if Stacy can play," I said.

She inhaled deeply and her eyes filled with tears. "Mahisha, you can't play with Stacy." She paused. My cousin Anissa, who sat next to me, took my hand. I didn't know what was going on, but I knew that I needed to go.

"Why not, mom? I won't stay out late!" I cried.

"Mahisha, Stacy was found in her closet. She is dead."

It took a moment for those words to register, but I finally said, "What? How? What happened?"

Another pause, then my mother said, "They say she hung herself."

I was stunned! I didn't understand, so I stammered out my words. "What. . .why. . . how. . ."

My mom held me while I wept. Looking back on the situation, I have my doubts. How did a ten-year-old figure out how to hang herself using a belt? Why would she do so? She seemed happy, most of the time. Was life so bad that suicide, at the age of ten, was the only way out? Did her stepfather kill her? Did she do this to escape?

I never got any of my questions answered. I didn't attend her funeral. I don't recall her mom even telling us about it. Every day, for the rest of the summer, I would look out the window looking for Stacy. Stacy was gone forever.

It was my mother's faith that helped me get through that trying time. My mother's faith in God has never wavered. God has always kept her, and us, through it all. "God takes care of his children," she would always tell us. I am the strong woman I am today because of her. She has exemplified what it is to be a woman on a mission, to make it happen, no matter how difficult life may be.

After being married for nearly two decades, she is newly single and enjoying life. I am happy she has finally found peace in her life.

That's really the story of most of my grandmother's children. They always find their way back to a peaceful place.

Everybody loved Uncle Kenneth, the former track star turned pimp, especially my brother and all of the boys and cousins in our family. I think it was because he always had a lot of money and he had women at his beck and call. All of the boys wanted to make fast money so that's why they all got involved in drug selling and hustling. It was a natural transition since all of the men in my family were hustlers.

It was sad because Uncle Kenneth had such a bright future ahead of him, had he stayed on the straight and narrow. He got invited to the Olympics but he just didn't make it. Then he ended up getting involved in prostitution and became a pimp. God has a way of turning things around though because Uncle Kenneth is now a minister and has an amazing new business.

My grandmother was a strong Pentecostal preacher. She was determined to make sure her kids were saved, and she raised her kids right but they all strayed away. Most of them, like my mother, eventually came back.

5
Coming Into My Own

My high school years were some of the best years of my life. Like most girls my age, I was boy crazy. Puberty had hit and I was no longer the odd, flat chested "church girl." I had pushed my date rape to the back of my mind and my dating prospects dramatically improved and I started to feel much better about myself. I had many male suitors beckoning for my attention. I think most of it stemmed from the fact that I was considered a challenge.

Everyone around school knew I was the virginal church girl that hadn't been "around the block."

My post high school plan was for me to go to Spelman College after completing two years of general education at Sacramento City College. But you know what they say about the best laid plans . . .

That boy craziness in me had intensified and when a handsome, charismatic young man named Roger approached me in the Student Union Center on campus, all plans to go away to finish college went right out the window. We got seriously involved and I never left Sacramento.

Roger was four years older than me, but I was young and in love. We were together for four years when I found out I was pregnant. Trying to balance school, a child, a relationship and money woes wasn't easy and soon took its toll on our relationship.

One day we had a horrible argument and he sent me home packing. I was several months pregnant with our child. With nowhere to go, I went back to live at my mother's house. That was one of the most stressful times of my life. I cried constantly.

I really wanted our relationship to work. I would ask him if we would get married and he would say, "Let's wait until after the baby is born, then we'll see if we stay together or not."

I was crushed. I wanted to get married and he wasn't even sure if we would stay together after the birth of our child? I felt alone, abandoned and unloved. I remember walking on my college campus, in my third trimester, with swollen feet, feeling fat, sad and alone....deserted by the man that impregnated and was supposed to be there for me. He left me to fiend alone. How could he do this to me?

I was so stressed during my pregnancy that many times, I thought I was about to go into premature labor. I knew that my child deserved better. I deserved better. So, I mentally worked at turning my mindset around.

My mom was crucial in that about-face. With her help, I was able to finish college. She was with me every step of the way. She was in the delivery room with me. She was there when I brought my daughter home to her house. She sacrificed her time and her schedule so that I could finish school and as a result of that, my mother and daughter formed a bond that is still strong to this day.

I went to school at night for two years and my mother would come home from work early to keep my baby. My daughter, Kiana was born in October—the middle of the semester, I took two weeks off and went right back to school. It took me longer to finish college but I finished. Then I started to really hustle. I knew that I had to change my life. I knew I had to change *our* lives. It wasn't a question of *if*, it was a question of *how*.

As I worked on my master plan—get myself together, finish school, and get a good job—I tried to get back in the dating game. That didn't exactly go according to plan.

One of the ways the date rape impacted me was through my self-esteem. For many years my self-esteem was so low that I didn't really expect much from anyone, or myself. I didn't feel pretty nor did I feel special. I felt inadequate and unworthy. So when my friend, Kim, who was dating a rookie on the Sacramento Kings, asked me to come along on double date with another player, I was apprehensive. I mean, what would I look like thinking a baller would want to go out with me?

But my friend wasn't going to take no for an answer.

"Girl, you HAVE to come out with me tonight!" she said. "He really wants to meet you!" she exclaimed.

"Kim, he doesn't even know what I look like," I replied. "You know how those guys are. They are really into the pretty girls."

She waved my comment off. "I told him what you look like! He is one of the starting players on the team. Google him. I did! He is fine!"

This conversation went back and forth for a while, until finally, I gave in. I was already out at a company party, dressed to the nines, so I finally said, "Fine. I'll meet you guys tonight."

I did like Kim said and Googled his name. I learned all about his NBA success and his career. I was nervous and excited all at once. *Will he like me? Am I pretty enough? Will we have anything to talk about?* So many thoughts and questions plagued me.

We all met up at a teammate's house. We spent forty-five minutes alone just talking and there was instant chemistry. We didn't kiss, we didn't have sex, we just talked and laughed. He was funny, charismatic and definitely good looking.

There was just one problem. . . I was still involved with Roger, Kiana's father. Still, I exchanged numbers with the baller and I thought that was the end of a fun night.

I couldn't have been more wrong. The very next morning he called me and asked if we could have lunch. This was the beginning of an intense love affair. I was on Cloud Nine and my self-esteem skyrocketed. To have a popular NBA star take notice of me, I was beyond excited. He could have any woman he wanted, yet he wanted me? Talk about finally feeling special!

I was also torn. Because the man that I wanted to marry me couldn't/wouldn't commit to me, even after having a child together. However, this popular baller wanted me by his side every day and at every game. I was smitten and I was game.

"Mahisha, we are playing the Lakers tonight," he told me one morning. "After the game we are going to meet at Morton's and a few players are going to meet us. Don't be late to the game and please wear that black dress for me." He flashed a wicked grin.

Of course, I worked that black dress that night as I was front and center (and on time) to watch my man do his thing.

That night, they beat the Lakers and my babe scored 20 points and we did go out afterward and hung with several of the players from both teams. It was a good night. There were many more nights just like that... until I found out the truth.

During the 1999 NBA playoffs, when I was on top of the world with my NBA baller, I made the heartbreaking discovery that my man was someone else's. Legally. Yes, my baller boyfriend was married.

The discovery came quite by accident. We had arranged to meet at a local club called Brandon's, with a few of his star teammates, for a night of dancing. I didn't ever want to come across as insecure (although I was), so I excused myself to mingle after being holed up in a corner with my boyfriend for almost an hour. Ten minutes after I walked away, my friend, Sasha (and the Club Promoter at Brandon's) grabbed me and pulled me in the back of the club.

"Mahisha, he has been talking to this woman since you left," she said. "She is all in his face. Follow me!"

After running up three flights of stairs, I noticed my boyfriend was sitting and chatting with another woman. And the way they were talking, it was obvious that they were intimately involved.

Furious, I walked up to him.

"I'm leaving," I said, not wanting to cause too much of a scene.

He jumped up just as I turned to walk off. He pulled me to the side.

"Babe, chill, okay?" He leaned in and kissed me. "I need to handle some business, go drop a teammate off and I'll be back. Just wait for me, okay?"

He didn't give me time to answer as he turned and headed toward the exit. The mystery woman, who had been glaring at me the whole time, stood and followed him out.

That was it. I lost it. I ran up behind him.

"Who is this woman?" I yelled. "Why is she following you?"

As the woman continued glaring at me, he calmly said, "Babe, I will be right back and I will explain."

"No! You tell me RIGHT now who she is!" I shouted.

He looked at me, shook his head, grabbed the woman's arm and led her outside.

Not to be dismissed, I followed them. I continued yelling, demanding answers, while the other woman was completely silent.

I didn't get any answers that night. They left together. I left ashamed, embarrassed and feeling like a fool.

Thirty minutes later, he started blowing up my cell phone. I refused to answer at first, but on the twentieth or so call I picked up.

"What?" I said, trying to keep my voice from cracking. I didn't want him to know how bad he had hurt me.

"Can we meet?" he asked.

"No."

"Babe, don't be like that."

"Tell me who that woman was!" I demanded.

Silence filled the phone.

"Tell me!" I repeated.

Finally, he took a deep breath and said, "That woman is my wife."

It felt like someone had taken a sledgehammer and slammed it into my stomach. I don't know why it hurt so bad, I mean, I was still involved with Roger. But there was something about that word, wife. Wife meant I was a mistress and I never wanted to be anyone's mistress.

"I don't want to be with her." His words made me realize that I was still sitting with the phone to my ear. "I want to be with you!" he pleaded. "We are getting divorced, I promise." As I wept, he continued. "I'm so sorry I didn't tell you earlier, baby. Don't give up on us. Come to the playoff game on Tuesday."

"Will she be there?" I found myself saying. I think I just wanted to hear his answer.

He hesitated. "Well, yeah, she is in town with the kids but. . ."

"Goodbye." I ended our relationship right then and there. A year later, they were divorced.

Once again, I was feeling like I got what I deserved. Karma had bitten me in my butt! I should have never entertained a relationship on the side without first ending the one I was in. That situation is the only moment in my life (of which I had control over) that I TRULY regret. I hurt Kiana's father more that I imagined. He found out about everything soon thereafter, and the events that happened after were truly brutal. He wept for days, vomited several times, wouldn't eat, didn't go to work for the entire week. I really hurt him. I didn't know how much he cared, until then.

"How could you do this to me Mahisha? How could you do this to our daughter?" he cried to me over and over.

My heart sank. I never meant to hurt him. I knew better, I was raised better. We both knew it was officially, and forever over. Kiana was going to be officially a product of a broken home, just like me.

My experience with the baller helped me to realize that I wanted to marry a regular guy, someone fabulous, yet regular, not a star, not an athlete. Someone I didn't have to share with the world. It was obvious that Kiana's father and I were not going to make it. So I continued dating, here and there. I was proposed to more times than I'd like to admit. But no one made a lasting impression. Then I met the love of my life. . .

He was a certified Microsoft Engineer from IBM contracted by Intel to work on a systems migration project.

I was talking on the phone with my girlfriend, Keena when I saw John for the first time.

I was on my way to the Intel Café to pick up lunch to take back to my office when I noticed him. We instantly made eye contact and my energy immediately changed.

"Who is that?!" I mumbled.

"Who is who?" she asked.

"Girl, let me call you back. I just met my husband."

"You are crazy." She laughed.

"Crazy in love at first sight. Bye." I hung the phone up with a quickness.

John didn't look like most guys in the office. Most of the guys at Intel were older white men, but John was young, sexy and had a hip-hop flavor that I was drawn to. I wasn't sure of his nationality. He looked Puerto Rican, but whatever his race was, I was smitten.

We met again at opposite ends of the salad bar. Every inch I took, he took. He looked up and smiled. I smiled. This went on all the way to the cash register. He followed behind me, after I paid my bill he approached me.

"Hello, my name is John. What is your name and what do you do here?"

My first reaction was, *Wow, did he really ask me what I do here as if I don't belong?* But I simply replied, "Well, my name is Mahisha Vernon and I am a Marketing Program Manager."

I could tell he was impressed and we ended up talking for five minutes. It was obvious we were enamored with each other. He told me that he was going to come by and see me since we both worked in the same building.

When I came back to work the next Monday there was a note in my office that read: *John from IBM came by to say hi.*

I was elated! I met him in the cafeteria later on that day and we ended up going out to dinner later that night. From that point on, we started dating and spending time together and we never stopped.

When we first met, he lived in D.C. but traveled to California for his project at Intel. He moved to California to be with me. We started talking marriage after three months of dating and got married a year and a half later. Thirteen years and three beautiful children later, we're still happily married.

Our journey hasn't always been easy. John is actually Korean and white and interracial dating can be challenging. I didn't feel the love from his parents at first, I think it was because I was black and I had a child. I'm sure they thought I was after his money, because he had a really great high-paying job. For one reason or another, they didn't attend our wedding. We had a small, surprise ceremony that took place in front of our bridal shower guests, nothing fancy. John and I chose not to have a big wedding, because he was very practical when it came to spending and I knew I wanted to branch out on my own and launch a business. I needed every dollar we had to do so.

6
Corporate Girl

As a young woman, I used to love Langston Hughes' poem, "Mother to Son," where he talks about how "life ain't been no crystal stair." That's because that's how I felt about my life. I'd had "tacks and splinters and boards torn up." Yet, I kept on climbing.

I'd made it out of the projects and was poised to make something of myself. I enrolled in Sacramento City College with a clear, well thought out plan.

When I got pregnant with Kiana, I was working at the Sacramento Blood Center as a receptionist. I was making next to nothing living paycheck to paycheck. I qualified for WIC, a program for women with infants that provided free infant formula, cheese, milk, juice and other basic necessities. I remember how it felt the day I signed up to receive my benefits.

"You know you also qualify for welfare," the social worker at the WIC office told me. "Honestly, you'd make more money on welfare than you do at your job."

I thought about what she said—and I thought about the countless people in my old neighborhood that did nothing with their lives but wait on the first of the month so they could get their welfare checks. No, that would not be me! I wanted to make my own way. Besides, I wanted the experience that came along with my job.

Two years later, I enrolled in California State University. While there, I applied for the internship through the CSU, Sacramento Co-Op department. I received a call in the middle of winter break with a rare opportunity for an internship in IT Marketing at Intel Corporation, a fortune

500 technology company. I wasn't exactly sure that it was the best fit for me, but I knew that they paid well and it would look good on my resume. Intel was a highly regarded in the industry, and honestly, I never expected them to call but they did. My interview consisted of me hosting a mock interview, after I had 30 minutes to write an article about the interview. The department head loved my writing style, and I was hired on the spot. This opportunity immediately changed our existence.

I excelled in my position and was excited about my future with Intel Corporation. I had an amazing job, doing what I enjoyed. I had a great manager, a great team. For the first time, I felt I had a bright future ahead of me. That flame was soon extinguished.

Internal promotions were common and expected. The average Intel employee changed positions every eighteen months. My next promotion landed me in America's Sales & Marketing Group. Three Managers later, I realized I had made a horrible decision.

One of those managers, Ethan Landers took issue with me from the moment he laid eyes on me. To this day, I'm not really sure why, but I have a pretty good guess. Before I went to work for Ethan, I thought I'd retire from Intel, be a good corporate citizen, and work my way up the corporate ladder.

When it was time for my first performance evaluation under Ethan, I received an extremely low score and I knew something was wrong.

Does not take direction.

Unable to process criticism.

Performing below her peers.

I remember reading some of those things, thinking, who is this guy talking about?

The things he wrote about me were ridiculous, because I took my job seriously and went the extra mile to do a great job.

"Ethan, can I have a word with you?" I asked him one day.

He acted like he didn't want to be bothered, but he motioned for me to come in his office.

"How may I help you?" he sneered. It was as if he knew he was messing with me and there was nothing I could do about it.

"I am concerned about my review," I told him. "I have performed consistently since I have been in this position. I am the ONLY Rep that has ALL of my clients trained, converted and using our new EDI system. I am the ONLY Rep leading the new Department initiative. I have helped create this initiative, outside of work hours. My accounts are all buying above allocated quantities. When my dad, uncle and Godfather ALL died within a two month span, I took a total of three days off! I am committed, loyal, dedicated to my job, my future. How could you do this to me?"

His eyes glazed over and he didn't respond. He simply slid a piece of paper toward me. I was forced to sign a Corrective Action Plan (CAP). Once you get on a CAP, it is understood that nine times of out ten, you were going to be let go. I was devastated, scared, worried. I had private school tuition for Kiana, a car note, rent. What was I going to do if I was fired. I broke down in my office and left early that day.

I took my complaint about the CAP and overall mistreatment to Ethan's superiors, to no avail.

I prayed about it every single day and honestly, every day I walked in the office, I wondered would it be my last.

I interviewed for four internal jobs and made it to the last interview on two of them. One manager admitted that she really wanted to hire me, that I was her first choice, but she couldn't. The things that Ethan said about me were so horrible that she couldn't justify it. I was beyond hurt.

About three months into my CAP, Ethan informed us that he was being promoted and would be leaving the country. All I could think was, *Thank you, Jesus, my prayers were answered!*

I immediately started to interview for other positions inside of Intel and received an amazing offer in EDM as a Marketing Program Manager.

On my next performance evaluation, I got an extremely high score. I received a raise, stock options, and an award. At that point it was even more evident that my poor reviews in the past from Ethan were fraudulent.

Ethan eventually came back to California. I ran into him in the Café a year later. He saw me, made eye contact, then moved to the other side of the Café.

I chuckled at his cowardliness. When I returned to my desk, I sent him an email with the subject line, 'My how things have changed.'

Dear Ethan,

Welcome back! I am glad to report that after you left I was offered a job in EDM. Not only did I get an amazing performance review, but I also got a raise, stock options AND an award. I am glad to know that ignorance isn't prevalent within Intel, only within a few bad apples. Thank you for teaching me an extremely valuable lesson.

God bless you!

Mahisha Vernon

He never replied.

Despite my rocky beginnings, I was proud to be at Intel. It was a great company, hard to get into, so the fact that I was an employee was quite an accomplishment. But when I dealt with that first experience of racism, I started looking at my future through a different lens.

Even though I had ultimately experienced success at Intel, it still bothered me that Ethan had tried to get rid of me and there was nothing I could do about it. I didn't like the feeling of dread that constantly hung over me. I didn't like walking into that building not knowing if security would greet me at the door with my belongings. I even had begun keeping my stuff together so I could easily clean out my desk with as little fanfare as possible if necessary. I hated that feeling. I hated the fact that I was fearful that all I worked for could all be snatched from me at a moment's notice.

I couldn't live like that.

I wanted to make sure that I wasn't in that vulnerable position ever again in life. I didn't want my destiny to rest in anyone else's hands and I knew that I had to do something to support me and my daughter no matter what.

That entire experience taught be that everything happens for a reason. Ethan was brought into my life to make my true destiny clear. Oftentimes we get bogged down in the stability of our career. We stifle our entrepreneurial voices because we like that direct deposit. But working for someone else means you will forever be at the mercy of someone else.

As someone who had fought and clawed her way out of the ghetto, that was not a place I ever wanted to be.

7
A Dollar and a Dream

A vacation changed my life. In April, 2001, John took me away to Santa Barbara for a relaxing vacation to celebrate my birthday. I had no idea that I'd come back poised to truly change my destiny.

We had a great time on the beach and just enjoying our time together. But it's something to be said about getting away from day to day life and stress that allows you to think clearly.

John and I discussed our future and I reiterated my desire to be an entrepreneur. I was scared about venturing out on my own, but I knew that I couldn't continue being an employee. My destiny was much larger than that. I knew that I wanted to start a business that could create sustainable income AND a future.

I remember John and I were laying out on the beach when he said, "You keep talking about wanting to do your own thing, it's time to stop talking and start doing."

"Oh, I couldn't agree more," I told him, leaning back to take in the gorgeous Santa Barbara sun. "I'm just not sure what kind of business I should launch." Since my specialty was marketing, I wanted to focus on a business that I could market well.

We sat thinking for a moment, then finally, John said, "What about something in the hair care industry."

This elicited a chuckle because my husband is half white and half Korean. There wasn't a lot he knew about black women's hair.

"No, I'm serious," he said when he noticed me laughing. "You have all these different products at home and none of them work for your hair. You're always mixing products at home trying to find the perfect mixture for your hair. I'm sure there are women across the world that have your same dilemma."

He was definitely right about that. From the time I was in the seventh grade until I was an adult, I relaxed and colored my hair. All of the processing had damaged my hair so badly, it would hardly grow. The process became so frustrating that I decided to let the relaxer grow out. I was going to go natural long before natural was popular.

My hair ended up growing long really fast and I was always in search of the perfect product for my hair. As I digested my John's words, I decided he was on to something. Natural hair care products would be the best products for me to market and that's how my business idea was born.

After coming up with a concept, I knew that I needed to come up with a name. The name had to speak to the product, be marketable and relatable.

That night, at dinner, John and I began writing the names of products down on a napkin. We started out with four products—shampoo, conditioner, a moisturizer and a styling crème. I decided to also launch a kid's line. There were four products in each line. (Now we have nine in the kid's line, fifteen in the adult line and we even have a baby line).

I returned to California, motivated and energized. I ended up getting laid off from Intel and because we still needed the money, I took a job working at Pfizer Pharmaceuticals. I had something to fall back on. I had money coming in. I needed a job that didn't require me being in the office all the time. I worked in the mornings from eight until twelve, then I would come home and spend the rest of the day on my business.

I was so hungry and excited to try something that I could do on my own. So for the time being, the excitement overrode the fear.

One of the greatest challenges I faced in getting my business off the ground was what a lot of budding entrepreneurs face—lack of capital. Since I did come from an impoverished background, I couldn't turn to family. Overcoming that lack of resources was a big challenge.

Again, though, that hunger inside me became more prevalent than my fear or my doubt.

Getting my business off the ground was extremely hard, not just because of a lack of resources, but just the overall struggle. At the beginning of my journey, I heard "no" a lot more than "yes." That was so frustrating, but I took that frustration, bottled it up and used it to fuel my determination.

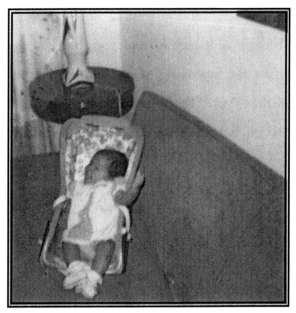

Me at 5 months old.

Me at 2 years old.

Me in third grade.

*Me and cousin
Keisha, Easter
Sunday.*

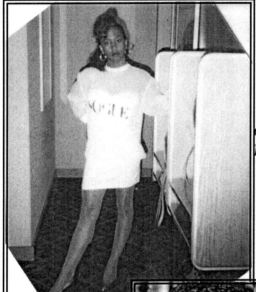

*High School
Graduation Night,
Valley High School.*

*Me and Kiana,
my oldest (4).*

My dad David Vernon.

My mom...

The night I met Mr. NBA.

With John, my husband, before we were married.

With Mom at my college graduation.

With my husband and four kids.

Family portrait—Mom, me, and my brother.

8
Success Story

I'm proud to be at the forefront of the natural hair care revolution. And while I am in good company, the success of CURLS is a direct reflection of the hard work and dedication I have to the business.

The business started as an E-commerce site. One hundred percent of the business was generated online. Then, salons started to call, then distributors, and then big box retailers.

I believe the key to a successful business is setting realistic attainable goals. If I had started out by going directly into big box retailers, I could've very well fallen short, and jeopardized the sustainability of my business.

Nowadays, if you walk the aisles of Target, Wal-Mart, Sally Beauty, or a host of other places, chances are you'll find CURLS prominently on display.

That's the direct result of years of hard work.

With the distribution expansion, CURLS continues to maintain the highest standards for quality ingredients and product dependability. I'm no longer mixing in my kitchen and in fact, I collaborated with leading cosmetic experts to develop my products. I have an intense desire to create a remarkable line for this growing, yet overlooked audience. This fact coupled with an extensive chemistry background, has proven to be a winning combination.

CURLS is recognized as a pioneer in the natural hair care industry. Continued development of new products has further established our position.

While CURLS continues to be one of the most recognized natural hair care brands in North America, our long-term strategic plan is to increase awareness among multi-ethnic consumers around the world.

Every year, CURLS grows and I see my vision expand. Our retail line is in Sally's, Target, and Wal-Mart and select CVS, Walgreens and Rite Aid stores. In addition to our retail line, we still have a professional line, which is available in salons for a higher price point.

The biggest challenge for a business like CURLS is competing with the big national hair care corporations. These are the white-owned companies with deep pockets and wide shelf space who put a label on a bottle and market it to African-American women. Our presence in the market has brought many of these companies to the natural hair care table, now that they see there is money to be made.

Keeping our core market while being authentic can be challenging at times. One thing remains unchanged is our commitment to quality. At CURLS we only produce quality products that our customers ask for. We are connected to the consumer after all, I am the consumer.

We're also very selective about the ingredients we formulate with. We formulate with certified organic ingredients and all of our products are sulfates, paraben, and silicone free. My mantra is healthy hair should also be beautiful.

CURLS is very active in the natural hair care community. We sponsor several events a month where we put our products in the consumer's hands knowing that they'll fall in love with them.

We offer product versatility. We have products for the full regime every curly woman needs. We also have products for every member of the family...baby, kids, and adults . . . cleansers, conditioners, moisturizers, styling products, and everything in between.

I'm going to be honest. It's a wonderful feeling to walk through the largest retailers in the country and see my products on their shelves. I still recall the day I got the call from Target that they wanted to carry CURLS products. It was a dream come true, and one that let me know my grass roots approach to marketing had paid off.

When I first came up with the concept of a hair care line, I knew that producing a great product was only half the journey. It did no good for me to have an awesome product if no one knew about it. I was also facing an uphill battle because this was the early stages of embracing natural hair care. The relaxer industry had done a phenomenal marketing job of convincing African Americans that silky straight was the way to go. So, I had to overcome that mindset, while building a product that challenged consumers to embrace their natural state.

I knew the way to do that was through grass roots marketing.

Grassroots marketing, sometimes known as guerilla marketing, basically means starting from the ground up. Instead of launching a message you hope will appeal to many people, you target your efforts to a small group and hope the group will spread your message to a much larger audience. Grassroots marketing often uses unconventional or nontraditional methods and often costs less than more conventional marketing efforts, but can yield big results.

I knew the first thing I had to do was target people or groups that I deemed influential. Those were people that when they talked, others listened. This could be in the form of popular bloggers, online magazines, YouTubers, and celebrities. I was counting on them to use their influence to spread the word about my product. For me, it was my hair care products. For a book author, it might be sending free books to Amazon's top reviewers in hopes they'll post favorable reviews about the book, which will then attract more readers, and buyers, to the book. A clothing company may give out a free item, with hopes that when the people get in the store, they buy something else. A restaurant might give away free or discount coupons to frequent diners, with the aim of having them rave to their friends and family about the restaurant's food.

Because these efforts are targeted to a small group, grass roots marketing often costs much less than broader marketing efforts and often features low-cost and free campaigns, such as posting on blogs, social media or message boards, holding giveaways and contests and other low-cost efforts. Rather than take out expensive print advertising to reach a broad audience, grassroots marketers can afford to launch several smaller-scale campaigns to reach separate defined audiences. Sampling proved to be a big win for us. Clients loved the 'try before you buy' concept. When you believe in your product, it's just a matter of getting others to believe as well. Providing samples—at events, meetings, trade shows—allowed me to do that.

Grassroots marketing is most effective if you can identify a definite market segment and appeal to the likes and dislikes of that segment. If you waste time marketing to groups who aren't interested in your product, or who have no influence with other groups, you won't gain from your efforts. It is important to develop a way to gauge the effect of a campaign, such as printing a coupon for people to turn in or counting the number of visitors to a website, can give you an idea of whether your efforts are paying off.

It's important to meet the consumer where they are. I know of an entrepreneur who started out the same time as me. This entrepreneur put most of her money into a big national ad. The high priced ad didn't generate many sales, and she subsequently went out of business.

When I started CURLS there wasn't Instagram, Facebook or Twitter, so I chose to do small advertising on targeted chat rooms and forums. I sponsored events, gave away a lot of samples. I met the people where they were.

You have to find creative ways to reach your market. Touch them, talk with them, engage them, show them the product, and let them sample the product.

I didn't have a publicist at the time so I had to do all of the groundwork. From there it got easier, but there was a lot of pounding the pavement.

That's not to say you can't get national coverage. You just have to be creative in your pursuit of it. My first magazine feature was in *Lucky* magazine. I secured this feature on my own and it took nine months of me going back and forth with the editor. I did a lot of shipping to editors myself. It was a lot of work and a long and tedious process, but the impact alone was phenomenal. That one feature resulted in an increase of $30-thousand dollars in sales for the month the feature ran. Back in those days, $30,00 was a lot for us!

It also gave us more visibility and was the catalyst for getting industry exposure.

Getting press of that magnitude can be more impactful than a paid ad. Having a trusted beauty expert declare their love for your product speaks volumes and helps build consumer trust, which translates into sales.

When you're reaching out to individuals, it's imperative that you do your homework. Find out who your contact is, but before you send your product to them, research how to create a creative pitch for your industry, make sure you stand out from the pack. Editors are busy, you want to make sure that you're not boring them with a typical pitch.

Eventually, my grass roots marketing efforts paid off—as word began to spread about my product. This was, however, only the beginning. A mature company cannot sustain on grass root marketing alone.

9
Having It All

Of course, creating a successful business doesn't come without a cost and if you're not careful, that cost can be your family.

A reporter once asked me what was the hardest thing about running my business. My answer is, and always will be, prioritizing family—making sure they don't suffer.

Any successful entrepreneur will tell you, having it all is a lot easier said than done. Building a business, a thriving business, requires long hours and lots of sweat equity. Even if you have a plethora of cash, the sweat equity alone can take a toll on your family. When I started CURLS, I mean, really and seriously committed to making it work, I didn't have enough balance. I worked way too much. That's why I'm thankful for my village.

A support system is crucial in building a business. Whether it's your parents, siblings, relatives, friends or neighbors, if you have a family, you simply can't go at it alone.

Two years after I started CURLS, I got pregnant again. John and I were so thrilled to give birth to a baby boy, who we named Bryce. Fourteen months later, Bryce welcomed a sister. Isabella, wasn't planned, but she was loved just the same.

The pressure of having a job, running a business, being a wife and mother to a toddler and a newborn pushed me over the edge. Like many other mothers, I experienced postpartum depression, but all of the pressures I was experiencing in life only made it worse. My doctor was concerned with my state, so he put me on medication for about four months and I was much better after that.

Fast forward five years and I had the urge to have another baby. Postpartum depression was definitely a concern because once you experience postpartum depression; you're prone to experience it again. I gave birth to our daughter, Kennedy and for the first few days after giving birth I was fine. Then Kennedy had to go back into the hospital because she had a severe case of jaundice. She was in the NICU for about a week and during that time, I went into a downward spiral and experienced postpartum depression again.

We caught it early. I started taking medication again and was fine. In a few months, I began weaning myself off the medication like I did before, because I didn't want to become dependent on any pills, but this time when I did that, things got worse. I had feelings I've never experienced before, severe depression and anxiety, I couldn't care for Kennedy without trembling. I tried to conquer it and shake it off, to no avail. I was bedridden for three months. I felt paralyzed. My poor husband was left to pick up the pieces.

It got so bad that my doctor told my husband that he was considering hospitalizing me. The doctor encouraged me to sell my business and do whatever I had to do to decrease the stress in my life. I remember that heartbreaking conversation with him.

"I've worked so hard," I told him. "And I love this company, but I love my family more. I'm going to have to sell."

We were sitting in our living room, snuggled under my favorite afghan. We had put the kids to bed and were supposed to be watching a movie. But we were so distracted that the movie was watching us.

John, who is one of the most caring men I know, was really concerned about my well-being. So, I fully expected him to support my decision.

"I don't know about selling, Sweetheart," he told me, causing me to look at him in shock. "I mean, you have put so much into building this company. It's not just your passion, it's your purpose. And you're just starting to build a name for yourself. I really don't think you should sell. You'll get through this. We'll get through this."

My love and respect for my husband went to a whole other level that night. And we did get through it. I didn't sell the business. For the next nine months, I continued seeing my doctor, making sure I was taking adequate care of myself. Eventually, I got better, much better. In fact, I was back to my old self and ready to be a mommy and a CEO. My village had stepped in at the most trying time, and they continued to be there as I continued to build my business.

Having a good support system is crucial. The beginning months, years of starting a business, heck, every day of running a business, requires a team of support to run a family, especially a family as large as mine. With four kids outside support is necessary. John is a great help, but we also have a nanny and my mother. . . a true team.

Even with that support system, I know there is an onus on me to make sure my kids get time with me. I can't begin to explain the number of times I have wished for magic powers so I could just stop the clock. Many days, make that most days, I feel like there simply aren't enough hours in the day to do everything that has to be done.

But no matter how hectic my schedule may be, my husband and I make sure we put our children first. As a team, we make sure that they have a TRUE childhood. We strive to strike a balance. Sometimes that means playing hooky from work so that we don't miss out. We spend our weekends doing activities that the children enjoy—going to the movies, the jump house, the park, or just biking, playing games, or dining out. The important thing is that we're doing these things as a family. While my husband and I both work, we make sure the children have a home full of love.

In the beginning, the amount of time I did work used to concern me. I used to feel like I was letting my business or my family down. But experience as taught me that my good enough is well, good enough.

Because I know that I am giving my all, working tirelessly on all fronts, I simply have to let go of some things. It is not humanly possible to do all the things my brain and my drive would like for me to do. And you know what? I'm okay with that.

As a working mother, you have to get to a place of understanding that your good enough is good enough. Although there is no secret recipe to balancing work and motherhood, there are thousands of women out there who have learned to do it successfully, women who've taken on this challenge before us and have come out on top.

If you ask most entrepreneurial moms, they'll tell you at one time or another they've had feelings of guilt. When we're working, we feel like we should be with our kids and when we're with the kids, we feel like we should be working. That's natural. And we shouldn't let that guilt stop us from striving for success in both work and as a mother. You can do them both and do them both well.

Of course there is no one size fit all solution to having it all, but I have found some common threads among successful entrepreneurial mothers.

Organization is key!

Nothing adds stress to your life more than trying to find an important file that is buried under mounds of paperwork. Or trying to remember what time the baby's doctor appointment is because you didn't write it down. You have to get and stay organized. Your work time is precious and not as dependable as it would be if you worked in a traditional workplace. You can't afford to waste time looking for files, sorting through junk mail or even finding a piece of paper to write on. Keep everything clean and organized from the start.

Proper planning.

Whether you use an old fashioned organizer or rely solely on your latest gadget, you'd be amazed at how a planner can help balance your work life with their family life, manage your daily tasks, and help prioritize your lie. (My personal favorite is my iPhone and all of the amazing applications for business owners). Of course, being flexible is key because at some point, your sitter will call in sick, your child will have a meltdown and your spouse may get called in to work.

Include the kids.

Sometimes, our children just want to be in the same room with us. When your children are little, child-proof your office and bring them in. Give them their own little space, and their own little tasks, and you'd be amazed, the kids will feel like they've gotten some mommy time while you've gotten some work done.

It's good enough.

Let's face it, we all weren't meant to be Barbara Billingsley, you know, the "Leave it to Beaver" mom who made lunches and homemade cookies for snacks? So what you had to go to the store to buy cookies for your daughter's class party? Your priorities are your family and then your work. Don't feel bad about being a store-bought cupcakes kind of mom. Find your 'good enough' and be happy with it.

Focus, focus, focus.

One of the challenges many entrepreneurial moms face is managing tasks while trying not to get sidetracked by children, laundry, dishes, etc. Make a list each month of what you intend to get done. Then break the list down week by week, then day by day. If you stay focused, you can stay committed to getting things done.

Ask for help.

It's very difficult to succeed without help, be it from your partner, family member or someone you hire. Communicate with your partner about how he can help you—you both need to remember you're juggling two full-time jobs. Figure out how to parent and chore-share so you're both on the same page. I have had to outsource

things (things that used to make me feel guilty), but I've learned that asking for help is essential to getting it all done. We have a housekeeper. I used to feel guilty about that. I had to finally tell myself that the amount of time it would take me to clean the house, given my daily workload and mommy duties, just wasn't worth it.

Don't forget about you.

In the grand scheme of trying to have it all, we often put ourselves on the back burner. It is crucial that you take care of *you*. How can you work out when you don't have enough time with your kids? How can you take a bubble bath when you need to make a presentation? Realize now that there will never be enough time in the day to get everything done. Your in-box will still be full when you die, so learn to accept that fact now. It may seem like a cliché, but in this case, it's the truth: You have to take care of yourself in order to take care of your family, your business and your home. If mama ain't happy, nobody is.

Finding that work-life balance is a never-ending quest. Research shows that the best mothers are happy, competent, socially connected, and supported—qualities that, for some women, are most easily attained by working a job they love. Since we know that if 'mama isn't happy, no one is,' make sure you do what makes you happy in your personal and professional journey.

10
Reflections

I have been asked, many times, how did I make it through all of my trials. I have never really been able to fully answer this question, beyond "I don't know. I just did."

Honesty, I am still plagued by some of my experiences. The date rape still haunts me to this day and has ultimately impacted every relationship I have been in, including my marriage to John.

The Bible says: *He that findeth a wife, findeth a good thing.* Well, my husband married a seriously scarred, damaged woman with baggage who still needs work, fifteen years later. He had to ceremoniously prove he was trustworthy, time and time again.

Not getting therapy was the biggest mistake I could have ever made. Sweeping hurt, pain, and abuse under the rug only temporarily pauses the pain. Instead, I should have dealt with it, head on because that was the only way true healing could ever take place.

I never felt pretty as a young girl, adult, or woman. I vowed that I would make an impact in other ways, to compensate for the areas that I lacked. I looked to others for validation. I am confident that my self-esteem issues are 100 percent connected to the rape.

Looking back at my experience with Mr. NBA, specifically, his desire for me, gave me a false sense of security and boosted my self-esteem. I gave him way too much power. His view of me, my hair (he preferred it blown straight vs. naturally curly), my clothes, my career all determined how I felt about myself. I loved me because he loved me. At least he loved the superficial me.

The biggest takeaway for me from that—Never, EVER let a man determine how good or bad you feel about yourself.

There's a saying that hurt people hurt people. At the time, I didn't realize how hurt I was. I didn't realize how deep the scars ran. Scarred people do not trust easily. My philosophy has always been, 'You have to earn my trust, you aren't automatically granted it!' While this protective shield has no doubt protected me from those that have meant me harm, it has also caused me to lose out on beneficial relationships. I have had to learn that not everyone is out to get me. I have learned to use my intuition and faith to guide me and not my hardened past.

Looking back on my life experiences I realize that God has truly blessed me beyond measure. I am not merely talking about the financial blessings, I am talking about the life-saving and life-changing blessings. I could have been killed in the drive-by, I could have gotten an STD and/or pregnant after the date rape, I could have led a life of despair, lacking love, light and opportunity. A few years later Mr. NBA was accused of abusing and holding a female companion hostage; that could have been me. While I focused on the dark side of all the things that happened to me, I failed to see the light. I failed to see the glass as half-full.

My journey hasn't been easy, it hasn't been perfect, but it is my journey and I am proud of the woman that I have become. Later in life, I started weekly therapy to help me on my path to healing. I have learned so much about myself, so much about life. I have learned how to love myself—flaws and all. Most importantly, through it all, I have learned to trust in Jesus.

11

The Wealth Mindset

I'm proud of my financial position in life, but contrary to what a lot of people may think, I never aspired to be rich. I wanted to be *wealthy*.

It wasn't always that way, though. I think there was a lot of fear driving me. Fear of being poor again; fear of going back to that impoverished life. I recently asked one of my mentors, who has a similar background, what drives him and he said the same thing—fear of going back to that poor lifestyle.

Being rich and being wealthy seem to be synonymous with success. However, there's a big difference between the two. If you notice, there are a lot of so-called 'get-rich-quick' schemes but there are no 'get-wealthy-quick' schemes.

The main difference between being rich and being wealthy is knowledge. Wealthy people know how to make money while rich people only *have* money. Rich people are motivated by money but wealthy people are motivated by their dreams, purpose and passion. Most rich people make a lot of money with their paychecks but the moment they stop working, they also stop making money.

Wealth, true wealth is often generational money, money that works for you, versus you working for money.

Most people do want to be rich. We want to enjoy the fruits of our labor and live a life that is more fortunate and ultimately extravagant than the average man. We dream of having the nice things. These are things that everyone wants, but very few actually get.

The difference between the ones that do and the ones that don't is not just simple luck. It's not the lack of opportunity that one person had behind the other. It comes down to the person, it comes down to their mindset, it comes down to their purpose, motivation and will power. It comes down to how bad they want it and how far they are willing to go. It's never the ones that are just motivated by money, it's the ones who are motivated to change the world and build a legacy because that is what wealth really is.

Rich just means having money. There are many rich people out there but not many of them are truly wealthy by definition. Wealthy people are not just rich in the pocket, but in the mind as well. They are the innovators and world-changers who have a significant impact on the lives of a great amount of people.

Rich people have money, wealthy people have assets.

Some people get lucky and land a high-paying contract, record a best-selling song, inherit money, or win the lottery. The rich spend this money or stick it in a money market account. Rich people may get money in an instant.

However, because of lack of proper mindset and poor money management skills, all of it can be lost in a short period of time.

Wealthy people invest the money in assets that keep making them more money. They don't just get paid a salary, they own the company.

As comedian Chris Rock once joked, *"I don't want to be Shaquille O'Neal. I want to be the man who writes Shaquille O'Neal's checks."*

Rich people acquire stuff, wealthy people acquire power. Rich people can afford to buy big houses, fancy cars, and lots of bling. But—as we often see in the tabloids—the money's often here today, gone tomorrow. Wealthy folks, on the other hand, invest their money in acquiring power and influence.

Chris Rock so aptly adds: *"Wealth is passed down from generation to generation. You can't get rid of wealth. Rich is some sh*t you can lose with a crazy summer and a drug habit. Rick James was rich. One minute you're singing 'Super Freak,' the next you're doing Old Navy commercials."*

Most people believe in overnight success. They think that if they could just put their mind to it, they are already half way there. There is so much more that goes into success than just believing you are worthy of it.

Think about how many people you see in the gym after New Years and then two weeks later you never see them again because they are not getting the instant results they want. That is the same thing that happens to so many people when they actually go out there and try to get the life they have always dreamed of.

Wealth is not something that comes out of nowhere and is just handed to you. Think about the difference between the guy that wins the lotto and the guy that actually worked hard for his success. The lotto guy ends up broke whereas the wealthy man will enjoy his success forever because he is not only strong in his pocket but in his mind as well.

His mind is what got him his success, not his good fortune. It's the ability to jump over the hurdles that are placed in your way and never stop chasing what you love that creates that mental wealth.

We often focus on the success that we see in others, but fail to recognize the hard work that led up to it. What you need to know is that everything worthwhile takes time. If you want to see incredible results and make incredible things happen, you need persistence and drive. Your ability to cultivate desire and take persistent action is what will make you successful, not your natural talents. It's all about consistent daily action.

Wealthy and rich people both may experience downfalls and failures in their ventures. However, because wealthy people are knowledgeable when it comes to money matters, they can start all over again and build wealth over time.

In contrast, rich people may find it hard to attain what he or she previously has. In essence, wealthy people are financially free while rich people are not.

Since wealth is not an overnight success, one must learn to distinguish an asset from a liability.

The key to acquiring wealth is to regularly monitor and increase your passive and portfolio income by increasing your means to earn and decreasing your expenses. The moment you decide to make the passive and portfolio income a part of your financial habit and discipline yourself in building it, you are on your way to financial freedom. This is the path in maintaining a strong wealth foundation.

Never forget that what you do on a daily basis determines your habits, and your habits determine who you are, what you accomplish, and the legacy you leave. People will measure you by what you do and what you have managed to accomplish in your lifetime, which then of course leads to your legacy. If you have inspired people and they are share and tell your story for generations to come, then you have created wealth in your life. You have left a legacy. You have done something different, you didn't settle for simply being rich.

You can tell the difference between a wealthy person and a rich person pretty easily. Most wealthy people don't stand out as much as the rich people. While the rich flaunt their money, the wealthy tend to live quieter but still adventurous lives. Rich people are motivated by money but wealthy people are motivated by their dreams, purpose and passion.

The definition of wealth is the number of days you can survive without physically working (or anyone in your household physically working) and still maintain your standard of living.

For example, if your monthly expenses are $5,000 and you have $20,000 in savings, your wealth is approximately four months or 120 days.

Ultimately, it's not how much money you make that matters but how much money you keep—and how long that money works for you.

Every day, I meet many people who make a lot of money, but all their money goes out of their expense column. Every time they make a little more money, they go shopping. They often buy a bigger house or a new car, or the latest designer trends, which results in long-term debt and more hard work. Nothing is left to go into the asset column. It's this kind of behavior that separates the rich from the wealthy.

I like the fine things in life just like everyone else, but my focus is not just on the "stuff." I'd rather focus on being smart with my money, working hard, and building a business and investments that provide enough cash flow each month to cover my expenses—including my fun liabilities like cars and houses.

I don't work for my money. It works for me. That's the key to separating the wealthy from the rich. While I am still working diligently on my plan to independent wealth, I am confident I on the right path.

12
Success Tips

Because of the success of my company, I'm often asked for words of wisdom from other aspiring and starting entrepreneurs. When it comes to making your mark, it's crucial that you stand out from the rest. It's essential that the business you are looking to venture into is something you're passionate about.

Being passionate has a direct application to business. It means having a strong feeling of enthusiasm or excitement for something or about *doing something.* A new entrepreneur will need this emotional charge to sustain his or her motivation when facing the unexpected challenges that all startups encounter. Passion will propel you forward when the going gets rough.

According to one estimate, eight out of ten businesses fail in the first eighteen months, so being passionate and prepared about what you're doing will likely be crucial for survival and success.

Surprisingly, a lot of people don't know what their passion is. For those that do figure out their purpose, most don't pursue the path to achieve it. Think of your passion as something you would do for free if money were no object. Do you know what your purpose is? Are you passionate about it?

The key to success is to clearly define your goals, understand your passion, and execute your life purpose. You must translate your dream of success into a series of small and large goals and differentiate them from wishes. A wish might be to co-direct a film with Steven Spielberg. An achievable goal might be to work with a Hollywood production company, which contracts out to Spielberg's films. Once you have attained your achievable goals, aim higher and put yourself on the position to reach those goals.

For the record, success isn't fueled by passion alone. There are many other factors that must be taken into consideration. Remember, there isn't one guaranteed path to success. My journey may not be your journey. However, I do believe that there are actions that, if done consistently, can help guide you to your gateway to success.

Here are just a few success tips to help you on your journey:

Learn the power of 'No.'

Let's face it, the door of opportunity doesn't just open up and welcome you in. If you're one of the rare people who thought up a business, set up a plan, then experienced success right off the bat, with little to no obstacles, consider yourself lucky. But for the majority of us, you will probably be told no a lot more than you are told yes. Never give up on yourself and never take no for an answer. I sincerely believe that my upbringing gave me extra strength in this space. I am one tough cookie! Yet, I still hate hearing the word 'no.' You must be prepared to hear "no" more than you will hear "yes" as a new business owner. The key is to keep marching toward your goal, past the rejection. Let the rejection fuel your determination. Power past the "no."

Don't go it alone—Get help!

I have to admit, asking for help used to be a difficult thing for me to do. It's one of the drawbacks of being a strong, independent woman. I quickly learned that by trying to go at it alone, I was doing myself a disservice. While it is important to know and understand all aspects of your business, it doesn't mean that you have to be the one to execute every task. It is true that we can always learn new things and become competent in them but what is also true is that we are only given 24 hours each day and to live full lives, it is more effective to do what we do best and to outsource tasks that we're not good at to people who excel at them. Delegating effectively takes trust and the ability to clearly communicate what you want.

Get a mentor.

I believe every professional should have a mentor and a life coach. A great mentor is invaluable. Common mistakes and business altering pitfalls can be avoided. I was able to tap into key contacts, vendors, expensive industry reports that were out of my reach. A great mentor will enable you to dramatically cut your learning curve. Mentors have gone down the road that you want to travel and can guide you to get to your destination faster than if you went at it alone.

Get a life coach.

Managing a demanding career with the day-to-day demands of a family like can be daunting. Having a life coach, someone to bounce personal challenges off has helped me through tough times.

Be Different.

Find your niche and stand out! Why blend in with the crowd when you can bring your authentic self, products, services to market? Figure out what your core competency is....what your key product/service benefits are and market your brand around them.

Know Your Weaknesses.

The sooner you realize that you cannot manage every task yourself, the better off you will be. Analyze your strengths so you can be aware of your weaknesses. Outsource talented people to perform in areas you are weak in.

Do your homework.

Before you launch out on your own to pursue your passion, do your due diligence. Research your industry inside and out. Understand what customers wants and needs....and deliver. Know your competitors. Test their products/services. Study your cost of goods before you undercut your profits.

Add Value.

No matter what you do and where you go, you can't go wrong with adding value. Simply put value is anything that people are willing to pay for. The more value you can offer, the more people will want your product.

Be Extraordinary.

If you do the same thing as everyone else, it's hard to be stand out. It is important to find a competitive edge and own it. That is how you become noticed and get what you want. How are you extraordinary? If you feel just ordinary, what are you going to do to become extraordinary?

Build a Support Group.

While mentors serve as a guide with whom you review your past actions and plan your next steps, a support group can be the companion that helps you out during the actual execution of your plan. This may be in the form of a mastermind group or accountability partner where you keep each other on track and accountable for your goals. It is extremely helpful to have someone you know that is willing to listen to your frustrations and self-doubt and to encourage you and remind you of how far you've already come.

Know the numbers.

Let's face it, numbers scare a lot of people. Start talking about assets, liabilities, gross pay and net worth and people's eyes just glaze over. If you are one of these people who run away from numbers, that's a habit you must immediately change. If you want to be financially independent, you need to know how to keep score. If you have your own business or want to successfully invest, your finances will tell you how well you are doing and reveal the health of a business. If accounting, profit and loss statements, balance sheets, and EBITDA calculations aren't your forte, hire a qualified CPA to help you manage your money.

Be Resilient.

Things rarely work out the way you planned and there will always be distractions and stumbling blocks that you have to deal with when you are on your road to success. The key point to remember is to persist and to develop the courage to move on even when everyone around you is telling you it is okay to give up. This does not mean stubbornly holding on to your original plan but rather continuing to pursue your goal as long as the reasons for doing so is still valid (make sure you know the "Why" of what you want). When everything seems to be going wrong, keep in mind that "the road to success is paved with a thousand failures" so each failure actually brings you closer to where you want to be.

13
Ready, Set, Go!

One of the most inspiring quotes I love is from motivational speaker, Les Brown. He says, "You don't have to be great to get started, but you have to get started to be great." This is the absolute truth. A lot of people have ideas to start a business, but the idea never goes any further than a thought.

I started a business in 2002 knowing very little about running a business. But I stuck with it, through post-partum depression, angst, lack of resources, failures and more. But none of that broke me. It made me stronger, and better.

There are so many people out there who have great business ideas...but zero confidence. They have all the tools they need to start an exciting small business, but they're so worried about following the rules and doing the right thing, about not offending people, or losing friends, or a million other irrelevant things, that they slowly but surely trample their exciting ideas into dust. Then, they spend countless hours trying to figure out why nothing great happens to them.

If you have an idea for a business, before you get hung up on being perfectly situated, or reading every business book in the market, or getting certified as an entrepreneur, stop talking about doing it, and do it!

You'll learn more in the first year than you would reading 1000 business books. Not to mention, while you're reading and contemplating and doubting and making excuses, someone else is out there *making it happen*. That's not to say educating yourself won't help, but too often, people get bogged down in preparing, that they never move forward.

Here are some tips to help you get started so that you can be great!

Learn from your mistakes.

You can read every business book and attend all the webinars in the world... but you're still going to have to get started. You're going to have to act. You're going to have to make your peace with not knowing what it means to own a small business—not even knowing what you don't know—and making mistakes. You can either decide that mistakes prove you're a bad, stupid person...or you can understand that mistakes are part of life. Mistakes are how you learn. Mistakes are how you grow.

Be realistic.

The small business owners who tend to succeed are the ones who understand their emotional triggers, and create coping mechanisms. They're the ones who learn from their mistakes, instead of allowing those mistakes to trigger their feelings of self-hatred, feelings that will, eventually, capsize their dreams. No matter how solid an idea you have, starting a business is so grueling that you must give yourself a fighting chance to succeed by eliminating as many pressure points as possible. For example, if you're working from home and your partner is currently paying the bills, causing your guilt to skyrocket, which in turn causes you to focus less on the business, and more on being the perfect domestic goddess. (A lot of women have wasted a *lot* of time worrying about their weight, their messy kitchens, what the neighbors thought, etc....when they could have used that energy to change their lives aka *the world*.) You're going to end up with a sparkling bathroom and a boring job working for someone else. Be cognizant of your emotions, and how they impact your productivity, and then join a co-working collective, or use a friend's spare bedroom, or rent a conference room in your local library. That way, over time, you'll feel less guilty and more purposeful, causing you to build a thriving business. With the fruits of your labor, you can hire someone else to scrub the shower. Even with the best of intentions, dreams are very hard to bring to life. Dreams are fragile. Identify your emotional triggers so you can avoid them, focusing your energy on the business, not your insecurities.

Take baby steps.

You can sit around, agonizing over everything, doing nothing, wondering if your business will flourish... or, you can commit to taking concrete, realistic steps every day to build your business. Of course there is no guarantee either way. But if you don't commit, if you're not consistent, if instead of constructive action, you spend your days beating yourself up about all the things that could go wrong...it simply won't work. It cannot work. You're going to have to take action every single day to make your business real. It can be overwhelming to have an idea and look around your small apartment and genuinely wonder, "How do I get there from here?" You get started by taking baby steps. Soon, you'll be soaring.

Be confident.

Business, and by extension, life is all about confidence. You can have an amazing idea, but if you don't believe in it, it'll never come true. It doesn't matter how many other people support your idea: *You* are the one who will do the hard work necessary to birth that idea. If you have a dream that you're passionate about, congratulations! You have everything you need to start a business that could change the world. Trust yourself. Allow yourself to present your ideas to the world in a confident manner that makes the world take positive notice. Confidence is especially important for all the women who, on the brink of world-altering ideas, hesitate and dismiss themselves, hoping that someone else will affirm them. If you wait for other people to hand you your affirmation, chances are you're going to waiting a very long time.

Why would you give away your power? Here's a better idea: give yourself that affirmation by bringing to life one of the many ideas in your brain.

Pamela Mitchell, founder and CEO of The Reinvention Institute, speaker and author of *The 10 Laws of Career Reinvention: Essential Survival Skills for Any Economy,* cautions that any business will have its ups and downs. The key to success is how you handle them.

"There will always be problems," says Mitchell. "Business is a series of solving problems. As much as you can, don't torture yourself."

She recommends staying focused on your current project or problem, solving that and remembering that things always shift and evolve. This does take some mental discipline, but it will help keep you grounded and moving forward.

Starting your own business is one of the most powerful ways to take control of your life and make extra money month after month. You can start with just a few hours a week. And best of all, *you* get to choose your hours, pick projects you find exciting, and meet interesting people.

Starting your own business isn't for the faint of heart. It's stressful and pretty much demands your complete focus. On the plus side, it can also be a fulfilling experience professionally and personally.

Here is some A to Z advice on how to make your business come to life:

A—Be willing to ADAPT.

If customers or investors reject your idea, don't let it get you down. Find out what didn't work, make adjustments and circle back to them when you've made the changes. Consider the possibility that the timing was wrong as well.

B—Write a BUSINESS plan.

Numerous studies have shown that one of the major reasons new businesses fail is poor planning. If you are planning on starting up a business, you must have a business plan. This will serve as a road map to guide you, and communicate with your bank and/ or investors what you're doing and why they should invest in you. A solid business plan will guide you going forward. Your business plan should include a mission statement, a company summary, an executive summary, a service or product offerings, a description of a target market, financial projections and the cost of the operation. Learn about how to write a business plan at SBA.gov.

C—Determine the COSTS.

Do additional research and find out what additional costs you will incur within your industry. Not only will this help you manage your business more effectively, investors will want to know this.

D—Don't worry about DILUTION.

So an investor has required a stake in the company. Recognize the fact that eventually at one point or another, you might face giving up some control of your business. Sometimes you have to bring in investors to take your business to the next level. The right partner, of course, is critical for continued success.

E—ESTABLISH a budget.

Once you determine how much money you'll have to work with, figure out how much it will take to develop your product or service and create a marketing plan. If you're selling a product, you must first determine the COGS (Cost of Goods Sold) before setting your retail price.

F—Be FLEXIBLE.

Chances are that your original idea will have to be modified. Being able to pivot and adapt to create what customers want will determine if your business will fail or succeed.

G—Write down your GOALS

What is a business without goals? Not just things you've haphazardly come up with in your head. Your goals should be well thought out and documented. Be as specific as you can when writing goals. Instead of, "I want to raise my company profile in the community," write, "I will volunteer my company's resources once a month to a specific community organization." Express your goals in positive words. Don't think about driving the competition out of business; think about how your product or service can fulfill an unmet need. And put time limits on your goals. How else can you hold yourself accountable?

H—HIRE the right people.

While this might seem obvious there are a few important guidelines to keep in mind. Mary Shulenberger, CEO of Parle Enterprises, Inc., a promotional advertising company in Brisbane, CA, says one of her first mistakes was employing family members, which caused problems when it didn't work out. Now she approaches hiring by making a complete list of qualities a candidate should possess. Shulenberger isn't afraid to demand the best, despite being a smaller company in a competitive market.

"Don't settle," she says. "There are qualified people out there, who might work for options or future opportunities. Be creative to get who you want."

I—Develop an IDEA.

Don't just start a business because something is in vogue and you think commercializing it will make money. Develop a business concept that you're passionate about related to something that you have experience with. From there, come up with a product or service that you believe can enhance people's lives.

J—JUST do it!

How long have you wanted to start your own business? A few months? A year or two? More than a decade? The world is full of two types of people; doers and talkers. Doers do. Talkers make excuses. If you have thought seriously about starting your own business but keep putting it off, it's time to move past these excuses and get on with achieving your dream and start your own business. Not sure if the idea is a good one? Go back to the cardinal rule, do your due diligence.

K—KEEP on track.

Your written goals should have a timetable to not only give you a road map, but keep you on target. But once you accomplish the goals on your list, don't rest on your laurels. Keep moving forward. Set new challenges. A successful business is always thriving and looking for ways to grow.

L—Determine the LEGAL structure.

Settle on which form of ownership is best for you: a sole proprietorship, a partnership, a limited liability company, a corporation, an S corporation, a nonprofit or a cooperative. Find out more at SBA.gov.

M—Identify your MARKET.

Even though you may have detected some interest in your business, you need to do more homework. Assess the market, targeting the customers most likely to make a purchase. Perform a competitive assessment, SWOT (Strength, Weakness, Opportunities, Threats) analysis, and conduct a focus group for input from your potential customers.

N—NETWORK.

Don't be afraid to get out there and network with other professionals, whether at a trade show, professional conference or at a local Chamber of Commerce mixer. The more people you meet that are connected in your industry, the more resources you have to pull from when in time of need.

O—Never be "OUT OF THE OFFICE."

Have you ever tried to connect with someone only to get one of those automatic "out of office" responses? Your business should always be accessible and open for opportunities. Not doing this costs you money!

That doesn't mean you don't take time off, just make sure clients and customers can ALWAYS get in touch with you, or an employee via a phone number, a website, a customer service email. No one should ever announce they are closed off to opportunities. They should be open for business no matter what.

I make sure that I give my family my full attention during my off hours. However, I make sure business is still being handled. Tweets are coming, Facebook posts are going out, and calls, texts and emails are still being answered. Even if it's by someone I've delegated that duty to. Always stay connected. We live in a 24/7 world. So even if you are going to be "out of the office," always be open for business, accessible and ready to do whatever it takes to satisfy customers, close deals and connect with others.

P—Be PATIENT.

Always keep in mind that success doesn't happen overnight. It's going to take some time before you make a profit. I was told that I could expect to be in the red (operating without a profit) for approximately three years. While we made a profit at the end of year one, I understood that my path to success would take time.

Q—QUESTION yourself.

Every idea you come up with won't be gold. Mistakes are part of the game. Don't be afraid to question yourself, or allow others to question you. You'd be amazed at what talking through an idea can do.

R—Use free RESOURCES.

Numerous free resources can offer advice, training and assistance. SBA.gov is a great place to look at to find local resources.

S—Get a great SUPPORT SYSTEM.

You're going to have to invest a lot of time and resources into your new business venture. Be certain that your family is on board. They must be aware that this process will be challenging financially and emotionally. You **need** a support system while you're starting a business (and afterward). A family member or friend that you can bounce ideas off and who will listen sympathetically to the latest business startup crisis is invaluable. Even better, find a mentor or, if you qualify, apply for a business startup program. When you're starting a business experienced guidance is the best support system of all.

T—Determine TAX obligations.

Now it's time to wrestle with the tax obligations. In the United States, four basic types of business taxes arise: income, self-employment, taxes for employees and excise taxes.

U—Arrive at a USEFUL definition of success.

Just because your business hasn't made you a millionaire (yet) doesn't mean that your enterprise is a failure. If you're able to make a profit doing something that you're passionate about, isn't that a success story?

V— Find the VALUE.

Maybe you've heard the saying "Love what you do and the money will follow." While this sounds nice in theory, it doesn't always work that way in real life.

There's no doubt that passion is an important key to success, but in order to build a profitable business, you need to offer something that others are looking for. After all, the market doesn't care that you're fulfilling your lifelong dream. People spend money on products or services that fill a need or desire. If there is no customer need, the business will fail.

W—Benefit from WORD-of-mouth.

Nothing beats good old-fashioned word-of-mouth marketing. Let friends, family members and influencers in your field spread the word about your product or service.

X—Go the eXtra mile!

Once you land a new client, be sure to go above and beyond the call of duty to make them happy. You'll have that customer hooked from then on. The cost of keeping a customer happy is cheaper than acquiring a new one.

Y— Do YOU!

The road to success is a hard one. But it's a lot easier if you're passionate about your business's purpose. If you don't love what you do, it's hard to be successful. If you aren't doing what makes YOU happy—not your mate, your family or your friend—the journey is much more difficult. Doing you helps you stay optimistic, which you have to maintain because once it's gone, you're done.

Z—Keep the ZEAL for your business.

This ends where we began. Make sure you have zeal for the one thing you must do to make your business succeed. If that's bringing in clients to your business, wake up each day with passion for serving your clients. Wake up each day with passion for reaching new clients and markets. Wake up each day with purpose. There will be many things that throw you off your game (the copier broke, a supplier didn't deliver, employees call in sick). Don't let that derail you. Keep the main issue on the forefront. Keep the zeal for what really matters.

Resources

No matter if you're looking to start or expand your business, there are many resources available to help. Be sure to check with your local minority associations and government offices for available services.

There are a number of available programs to assist startups, micro businesses, and underserved or disadvantaged groups. The following resources provide information to help specialized audiences start their own businesses.

Small Business Administration

www.sba.gov

Here you can learn how to start your own business and finance it. The site also provides information on business opportunities, local SBA offices, laws and regulations, and much more.

Entrepreneur Magazine

www.Entreprenuer.com

Entrepreneur Magazine's website has a gem for entrepreneurs: startup kits. There are kits for everything from starting a restaurant to a consulting firm, complete with articles, guides, marketing tips, and more.

eHow's Introduction to Entrepreneurship
www.ehow.com

Collaborative knowledge resource website eHow has hundreds of thousands of great articles, including a strong set of guides and resources for how to open a business, how to incorporate, raising money, and bookkeeping.

Salesforce.com

www.salesforce.com

Easy-to-use web-based customer relation management tools for your entire company, including online solutions for sales, service, marketing, and call center operations.

14
Loving My Curls

Of course, no book about me would be complete without hair care information. Hair is my business. Not just because it's something I'm passionate about, but because I really do make it my mission to help women embrace their natural texture.

The decision to forgo your long-term relationship with your chemical addiction of choice (relaxers, perms, and straighteners) is one that tends to cause more heartache and turmoil then the current economic environment. But "Transitioning" has become commonplace in the ethnic community. According to a recent Mintel report, more than 10 million ethnic (African American, Hispanic and Asian) women have also decided to join the natural revolution and embrace their natural kinks, waves, and curls resulting in a dramatic decline in the sales of relaxers. Mintel expects sales to drop even further this year, to an estimated $152 million as African-American women increasingly opt for styles that don't require them to chemically alter their natural curl pattern.

The Mintel report found that, "nearly three-fourths (70%) of Black women say they currently wear or have worn their hair natural (no relaxer or perm), more than half (53%) have worn braids, and four out of 10 (41%) have worn locs."

This report marks a real shift in African-American beauty culture, and is something of a resurgence hearkening back to the 'Say it Loud, I'm Black and I'm Proud" days. (Who can forget Pam Grier and her to-die-for Afro as Foxy Brown?).

When the activism of the '60s and '70s gave way to the assimilation of the '80s, Afros soon disappeared as African-American women returned en masse to relaxing their hair. I was among those who believed that straightened hair was the epitome of beauty and professionalism.

I got my first perm when I was 12 years old. Like most of my friends, I was 'conditioned' to believe that loose waves and straight hair trumped tightly coiled tresses. My best friend's mother applied the creamy crack to our mid-back length hair, twenty minutes later we had perfect curls—loose and shiny. It was love at first sight! I was addicted.

Soon my obsession with the "perfect curl" led me to find the perfect auburn hair color to accent my caramel skin. Needless to say, DIY hair dye and chemical relaxers kits do not mix! Six months later my mid-back length hair was below just my ears. That didn't deter me. I kept up the same song and dance throughout high school. My hair was so thin you could see right through it when it was down. I decided to go natural shortly thereafter. I stopped relaxing and cut off four inches to start. The process was long. I spent two years transitioning and I kept my hair in a bun to control the two different textures. At the end of the journey I had a head of full, tightly coiled perfect tresses…healthy and strong. I never went back!

The concern over the lack of easy and professional styling options have caused a bit of uncertainty for some. Rest assured there are a host of resources, quality products, and transitioning specific resources to help.

Before you begin your journey to shedding the "creamy crack," as relaxers are commonly known in the African-American community, you must decide where you want to start. You have a few choices:

1. You can grow out the chemicals (which takes the most time and patience),

2. Cut off all of the chemicals at once and rock your TWA (transitioner's slang for teeny weenie afro), or

3. Cut half of the chemicals off and get regular trims (three to four inches) every three months to speed up the process.

Very important note: the point where your natural and your relaxed hair meet is THE most vulnerable . . . therefore is more likely to break if not properly handled and taken care of. You want to keep your hair well-conditioned and hydrated to ensure a smooth, breakage free transition.

If you are ready to make that leap, here are a few key steps that you must commit to:

1. You definitely want to start by giving yourself a weekly deep treatment with heat for the next few months. Invest in the Hair Therapy Wrap, now available at www.curls.biz (and a few plastic caps to cover your hair). This portable invention allows you to do chores, check email, etc., while conditioning at the same. You no longer have to sit under a hot dryer or go to a salon for deep treatment…with a Heat Therapy Wrap

you can do it yourself! Your hair needs a conditioner that is geared to replenish chemically altered hair. CURL Ecstasy Hair Tea conditioner will transform your dry, chemically damaged, overstressed tresses within minutes! This magical Asian tea formulation combines natural botanicals and vitamin packed extracts with rich, exotic emollients to moisturize, condition, strengthen and protect your delicate locks.

2. It is imperative that you moisturize your hair daily. CURLS Quenched Curls moisturizer a great option. It softens the hair, eases comb ability, moisturizes and conditions, preps it for the next step, and leaves a little goodness behind. Use this daily.

3. Over shampooing (with traditional shampoos) and under conditioning are common culprits for dry, breakage prone hair. Therefore, shampooing more than one time a week is not recommended. On the other "shampoo-less" days do a conditioning rinse—

rinse hair to remove styling products (this is where using the right products that are water soluble come in), apply an ample amount of conditioner, comb through, rinse and proceed with styling. Doing so will pump much needed moisture back into your hair (without stripping away essential nutrients), rinse away unnecessary dirt and oil and give you a fresh clean start. I recommend using sulfate free cleansers at all times.

4. Using the right products, with quality ingredients is absolutely necessary. Avoid products with mineral and/or petrolatum oil in them . . . as both of these synthetic oils coat and suffocate the hair shaft, blocking moisture out thus drying out the hair. Remember, dryness leads to breakage. If applied directly to the scalp, mineral and petrolatum oil can actually retard growth. If your hair requires oil, always opt for a natural oil such as olive, jojoba, coconut, almond oil, etc. These natural oils actually penetrate and moisturize the hair.

5. Avoid drying products such as gel, hairspray and mousse with drying alcohol. If you need curl enhancement, opt for curl enhancers, lotions and creams.

6. Reduce the amount of times per month you heat process your hair. If you currently are doing so three times a month, cut back to two times a month with a goal of once a month MAX! This will ensure the health and integrity of your hair.

7. Make sure you get regular trims. . . starting off with an inch or two is a great idea!

Millions of women still choose to perm their hair. Or more and more, choosing protective styles. The market for hair extensions—including synthetic and human hair,—continues to grow.

But whether you're loving your natural curls on full display, or keeping them protected under the latest protective style, you still want to make taking care of your God-given tresses a priority.

15
Health Care Tips

As most naturalistas will tell you, taking care of your hair can more often than not, be easier said than done.

Tame the curls

Curly hair is the most temperamental textured tress on this planet. Frizz from touching the hair too often, limp noodle curls from over conditioning, dry, straw-like curls from under conditioning or over shampooing, and seasonal changes that make us wonder, "What on God's green earth has happened to my beautiful curls?" are all common curly girl experiences.

You can help your hair with these rehab tips:

1. Strip, but don't tease! Start with a clean palate every three months, especially you product junkies that just can't seem to say "no" to any product that is curl related. Try a "CURLS Detox" cleansing as a part of your rehab. Choose a clarifying shampoo that is ph balanced and contains mild surfactants to avoid over drying the hair. I recommend our Pure Curls Clarifying Shampoo.

2. Product Relativity—While some curlies like to "cocktail" two or more products together to create the perfect coil, I advise against mixing styling products from different product lines. Oftentimes, active ingredients will collide and cause the white ball effect

or harden up on the hair. Try one product line at a time.

3. Defrizz & Debunk! Debunk the myth that the more products applied on the hair the better the curls. The truth is, the number one cause of frizz is product overload. Simplify your styling regime.

4. Use sulfate free cleansers to ease dry, brittle hair and ends. Sulfates are harsh detergents that cause the suds factor in your cleanser and results in dry hair. I recommend our Curlicious Curls Cleansing Cream.

5. Stop heat styling altogether. The excess heat further exacerbates the problem.

6. Deep treat your hair with a super hydrating, natural based deep conditioner. Add heat so that the conditioner actually penetrates the hair shaft. The portable microhaircap is ideal for conditioning on the go! This cordless design enables user to walk around during treatment.

7. Moisturize daily...remember, this is key to healthy hair!

8. Add a natural oil of your choice (e.g. pomegranate seed, olive, jojoba, or sunflower oil) to your styling products for extra moisture. You can purchase natural oils at your local health food store.

9. Be patient with slow growing hair. Realize that all hair grows, on average, ½ " per month. African American hair grows at the same rate.

10. Take a multi vitamin full of rich minerals and drink eight glasses of water a day.

11. Use products formulated with proven growth enhancing ingredients (e.g. MSM, Silica and Lecithin)

   ➤ Dr. Stanley Jacob and Ronald Lawrence treated more than 1,000 patients with MSM for everything from osteoarthritis to allergies to Seborrhoeic Dermatitis and arthritis. **When it**

came to hair, they reported that 100% of their patients taking MSM experienced increased growth. MSM (methylsulfonylmethane) is a naturally occurring nutrient, a sulfur compound—an important element for a healthy scalp, and the growth of hair and nails.

12. Get a weekly scalp massage to provide stimulation to the hair follicles.

13. Restore your hair's lost keratin. Ninety percent of human hair is made up of a natural protein, keratin, which is responsible for the hair's strength, resistance to wear and tear, elasticity, flexibility and shine. Hair keratin is damaged by straighteners, colors, perms, blow-drying, the sun, pollution, pool chemicals and even everyday brushing. Seek out products that are keratin based to restore strength and elasticity. Sweet and sour—honey and vinegar—the key to frizz free hair.

14. Pucker up to beat the fizz. A distilled white vinegar rinse is a great addition in the shower. The technique is fast and easy and requires one common household item.

    a. Rinse hair with warm water to remove product. Skip shampooing. Apply vinegar directly to hair and scalp. I like to use a bottle with spout top for easy distribution. Gently massage. Rinse. Condition as usual. Not only is vinegar great at reducing frizz by sealing the cuticle by restoring it to its natural ph balance, but it also removes build-up and adds sheen, leaving tresses feeling soft as a baby's bum. WORD OF CAUTION—avoid over indulging in this quick fix, straw like tresses will be the result. Do so once every two weeks for the best results.

    b. Honey is also a great natural remedy for combating frizz. Mixed with a little conditioner (for fine hair) or applied directly to your hair, after shampooing and before conditioning.

There are times when you want to wear a good ole' blowout and that's okay! It's good to change up your style game. Follow this step-by step guide for the perfect blowout.

Shampoo and deep condition your hair

- Begin by thoroughly cleansing your hair and scalp. You should never use heat on dirty hair. Doing so could cause your hair to accumulate a build-up on the exterior of your strands, which could be more difficult to remove. Next, fortify your strands for added strength with a deep conditioner. It is always good to strengthen your hair before applying any form of heat to your hair. Heat has the ability to deeply damage hair strands, penetrating all levels of the hair. Therefore, cover your bases by cleansing, enriching and strengthening your hair before *and* after heat styling.

Get a heat protectant

- A heat protectant will not prevent ALL forms of heat damage but it will help you and your strands from excessive heat damage. You could also use a high quality oil with your blowout to protect while blow drying. High quality oils and heat protectants serve as a barrier between the heat and your hair. They shield the hair from the high, harmful temperatures, while still allowing for the temporary change of hairstyles.

Use Attachments

- If you have kinky curly hair, use a comb attachment to smooth your hair and speed up drying time. The comb allows for more air to blow throughout large sections of your hair. This makes changing your hairstyles for curly hair a breeze, as it is detangling while drying. Other hair types can also use a comb attachment or they can use a nozzle with a round brush for a more voluminous blowout.

Do not blow dry sopping wet hair

- Allow your hair to dry a bit before styling, or try to remove excess moisture with paper towels or a micro fiber towel. You can also allow the hair to air dry before beginning your styling process. This technique also allows for a shorter time span of heat styling, which is healthier for the hair.

Blow!

- Part your hair in small sections. Each section should receive a dose of your favorite leave-in conditioner or moisturizer, followed by your heat protectant or luxury oil. Blow dry your hair in small sections beginning with the back section. Once complete, secure this section with a hairpin and allow it to cool. Remember, once the hair is dry, do not continue blow drying over that section, simply clip it out of the way and move on to the next section.

Extra care for curly gray hair.

- Curly hair has a tendency to be dry, due to the many twists and turns it takes your natural oils to travel down to keep your hair protected and hydrated. Gray hair adds another challenge on top of that; coarse texture. Gray hair tends to be wiry and difficult to manage. Whether or not you are already rocking your gray curls or they are slowing growing in, here are some tips to help you cope!

1. Go crazy with conditioning—If you usually condition once a week, double that. If you deep treat once a month, upgrade to twice a month!

2. Take moisturizing to its heights—Evening moisturizing should be done daily with Lavish Curls Moisturizer before applying your silk scarf or bonnet.

3. Choose an adequate styler—You may need extra control in your styling aids. Blueberry Bliss Curl

Control paste can adjust from soft to firm based on adding water to your styling.

Taking care of your children's hair

Children live very active lives. Like us, they rise early in the morning and prepare for their day. Some of them go to before school programs, and then endure a full "work day" of school followed by homework time or after school care activities and sports. With a day like that, it's no wonder they come home with dry hair, even after you carefully moisturized their strands that morning. Your child needs something that will last them the full day. Now this doesn't guarantee that their hairstyle will last, but it does mean their hydration level will remain intact.

The L.O.C Method is one way to keep your child's hair curly hair fully moisturized.

L—Leave in Conditioner

After Cleansing and Conditioning your child's curly hair, apply a leave in conditioner for kids like CURLS Curly Q Moist Curls-Curl Moisturizer/Detangler to your child's strands and finger comb throughout or use a comb if you wish. This process is very important as the leave in conditioner will remain on the hair. Leave in Conditioners are light but have just the right amount for a daily dose of moisture.

O—Oil

The next step is to apply an oil. The Mimosa Curly Q Elixir is the perfect oil for children's hair. Apply this oil after applying the leave in conditioner. The oil in this process acts as a sealer. It has moisturizing elements also but it will seal the moisture into the hair before any styling is done to the hair.

C—Cream

The final step is applying your cream stylers. You may also use a gel if that is what is best for your child's hair. This is the last and final step because once your child's hair has been properly moisturized it is prepared to behave during the styling process. I recommend our Curly Q Custard.

Keep a close eye on your child's **curly hair care patterns** to see what is best for them. This method can actually be done every day or as needed.

For babies, the hair care regimen is just a tad bit different. A baby's hair can sometimes be a bit tricky to work with. The early stages of hair growth for babies can differ from baby to baby, mostly due to genetics. The most important thing early on is caring for the scalp of your baby. The scalp is trying to regulate itself from the womb to the world and it sometimes has a challenging time adjusting to the air and the moisture that we are so accustomed to. Start your baby off with a line of the best organic hair care products formulated for babies. Organic products are gentle, and effective. Once you have made that selection, you are ready to go.

Here are some suggestions for how to care for your little baby's hair:

Scalp

Cradle Cap affects a large number of children for different reasons. So, caring for the scalp has become increasingly important. Cleanse your child's hair when you see dry or oily scalp. The first nine to twelve months marks a period of regulation of oil production, so you may need to assist the process along. You can cleanse no less than once a week and no more than every other day. Follow with a compatible conditioner and massage the scalp very gently. You can apply oils before or after cleansing your baby's hair for added moisture.

Hair

You will notice that most baby hair holds a great curl. Infant hair tends to curl because of its fine and lightweight nature. As time progresses, the hair will become stronger, thicker and typically darker based on genetics. Sometimes you see delayed hair growth, which is also based on genetics or could be as a result of the baby laying down. Be sure your baby gets tummy time daily to help prevent baby baldness due to laying in a car seat or bed. If your baby struggles with growth after two years, see a specialist. Care for the baby's hair with gentle conditioning creams, moisturizers and oils as needed.

The total experience

Be kind to your baby by caring for every inch of them. Make your bath times special by playing with toys and singing songs, then end your bath time with your cleansing and conditioning session. For daily styling, use your moisturizing and conditioning creams and twirl the curls around your fingers. Smile and laugh with your baby and have fun throughout the process.

What not to use

Surfing the shelves of the decadently designed beauty counters can be as challenging as attempting to explain the latest theory on Quantum Physics. Some of the ingredients listed on the bottle of your favorite luxury shampoo may even sound like they belong in a scientific equation. Try saying Methylchroloisothiazolinone! Did you know that this commonly used hair and skin care preservative has been under attack and accused of being carcinogenic? While I do not subscribe to Internet "hair care ingredient scare" hype, I do believe, 100 percent, in knowing what you are putting on your hair. Here is an introductory look into some of the common hair ingredient pitfalls, myths, and untruths.

1. **The alcohol debate**—I am often asked about alcohol and hair care products. Many people believe that alcohol, which is a family of chemicals, is drying for the hair. This is an example of a case where a little knowledge can be misleading. *TRUTH*— *Some* alcohols are extremely drying and damaging while others are fatty, emollient conditioners. There are literally thousands of different alcohols used in different products for different reasons. So when you're looking over product labels, it is important to know a little more about the specific type of alcohol in the product in order to make an informed decision.

EXAMPLES OF DRYING ALCOHOLS—All of these alcohols are drying to skin and hair. They are commonly found in hairspray, mouse, and gel products.

- o Ethanol alcohol,

- o Isopropyl alcohol,

- o SD alcohol

- o Ethyl alcohol

EXAMPLES OF HEALTHY ALCOHOLS

a. Cetearyl alcohol—This naturally derived alcohol provides the creamy consistency that makes hair products easier to distribute the product through the hair. This is an especially beneficial ingredient in Black hair products because it also lubricates the hair making detangling a snap.

b. Cetyl alcohol- This is a fatty alcohol that is derived from coconut and palm oils. Far from drying, this emollient makes hair and skin softer.

c. Stearyl alcohol—another fatty emollient and moisturizer.

1. **The truth about mineral and petrolatum oil—** The best oil for your hair is always a natural oil. I personally prefer using pomegranate seed, jojoba, coconut, and almond oil for my hair. The traditional hair grease we all grew up using on our naturally curly, kinky, textured, and afro styled hair is made of mineral oil and/or petrolatum oil. Avoid products with these oils in them...as both of these synthetic oils coat and suffocate the hair shaft, blocking moisture out...thus drying out the hair. If applied directly to the scalp, mineral and petrolatum oil can actually retard growth. Mineral oil is a derivative of crude oil (petroleum) that is used industrially as a cutting fluid

and lubricating oil. Petrolatum—A petroleum-based grease that is used industrially as a grease component. Petrolatum exhibits many of the same potentially harmful properties as mineral oil.

2. **Parabens cause cancer . . . myth or fact?** There have been many studies, presented on and offline about the heath risks of using products formulated with a parabens (a preservative used in cosmetics to protect the user from the growth of microbial organisms). The paraben opponents argue that this commonly used cosmetic ingredient, causes cancer, by mimicking the hormone estrogen. A study published in 2004 documented that it found parabens in breast cancer. One downfall of the study is that it left many unanswered questions...questions relevant to the significance Others say that it is 100 percent safe...arguing that while parabens may act similarly to estrogen, the body naturally produced estrogenic activity far outweighs the threat of any cosmetic product. What do we believe?

Here is what the FDA's website stated on parabens.

The Cosmetic Ingredient Review (CIR) reviewed the safety of methylparaben, propylparaben, and butylparaben in 1984 and concluded they were safe for use in cosmetic products at levels up to 25 percent. Typically parabens are used at levels ranging from 0.01 to 0.3 percent. In December 2005, after considering the margins of safety for exposure to women and infants, the Panel determined that there was no need to change its original conclusion that parabens are safe as used in cosmetics. www.cfsan. fda.gov/~dms/cos-para.html

16
Recipes

Of course, since I've spent a great deal of the book talking about following your passion, I have to close by telling you a little bit about mine.

You know about the success of CURLS. But there is a reason for the success. Besides the blueprint I've laid out, of strategic marketing, commitment to customers and a business-savvy mindset, we simply make a great product.

Whether it's springy, spirally curls, or sexy, loose curls you're after, CURLS has the perfect products to get your locks under control and in curl-tastic shape. The curly girl's secret weapon is out, CURLS is a line of premium hair care products that cater to today's growing demand for effective, luxurious and natural products.

CURLS has the perfect products for all curly hair types. With a complete range of cleansers, moisturizers, conditioners and stylers, there is a curl regimen just right for you. Our products are made with an exclusive blend of natural oils and plant extracts to nourish dry, damaged curls. This magic curl concoction includes *Monoi de Tahiti*, which hydrates and restores shine and bounce, *green tea extract*, which soothes and moisturizes, *soy protein*, which strengthens and reinforces the hair shaft, and *avocado oil* and *pomegranate seed oil*, both of which are excellent moisturizers that contain high levels of vitamins A, D & E.

As any curly girl knows, not all curls are created equal, so I have created a regimen for every type of curly hair, taking into consideration that often there are multiple curl patterns in one head of hair.

Kinky Curls

- Start your regimen off by cleansing with **Curlicious Curls Cleansing Cream**. This thick and rich, sulfate-free cleanser is gentle enough to use daily and moisturizing enough to use alone on its own. It's ideal for chemically altered and color treated hair.

- After rinsing, condition with **Coconut Sublime Conditioner**. This delicious treat is guaranteed to soften the kinkiest curl, moisturize the driest lock, and detangle the most unruly tresses. The secret to such amazing results is pure coconut milk.

- Now indulge your curls in the **Curl Milkshake**. This creamy curl reviver will soften your curls and leave them smooth as silk. Made from pure coconut and sweet almond milk, this delectable delight is truly one of a kind and is my personal favorite.

- If you like to style your natural or kinky curls in twists, locs or straw sets, **Whipped Cream** is the product for you. It defines, defrizzes, moisturizes and holds curls. This cream will elongate curls and has a warm vanilla cream fragrance that will keep you coming back for more.

- To keep curls looking their best, treat them once a month with **Curl Ecstasy Hair Tea Conditioner.** This must-have conditioner combines exotic extracts and vitamin packed botanicals with natural emollients to moisturize, condition, strengthen and protect over-worked curls.

Curly Curls

- Start your regimen off by cleansing with **Curlicious Curls Cleansing Cream.** This thick and rich, sulfate-free cleanser is gentle enough to use daily and moisturizing enough to use alone on its own. It's ideal for chemically altered and color treated hair.
- Rinse and then condition with **Curl Ecstasy Asian Hair Tea Conditioner,** leaving in about ten percent for continued protection.
- For extra dry curls, **Quenched Curls Moisturizer** is an exceptional moisturizer that hydrates, conditions

and revives curls, restoring their natural beauty. Consider this your "underwear for your hair."

- Follow up with the **Curl Gel-les'c**, a brilliant styler, which imparts a healthy sheen, banishes frizz, and defines curls with a medium/strong hold. It works wonders for thick, frizzy curls.

- For a softer look when putting curls back in a ponytail or bun, grab the **Curls Milkshake**.

- If you prefer extra hold, the **Curls Goddess Glaze** is frizz-fighting, curl enhancing, botanical gel that promotes shine and will leave locs looking flawless.

Loose Curls

- First, cleanse with the **Curlicious Curls Cleansing Cream**. This gentle cleanser will hydrate while it cleans the hair and scalp of products past without stripping away essential nutrients.

- Apply **Curl Ecstasy Asian Hair Tea Conditioner** and let it sit for approximately five minutes before rinsing.

- After conditioning, comb a dime-size dollop of the **Curls Milkshake** throughout curls, letting hair air dry.
- To go from loose curls to springy ones, the **Curls Goddess Glaze** is a botanical gel that will create frizz-free curls.

Of course, it's great if you let me do the work for you and provide you with great products at your fingertips, but sometimes, you may want to play chemist yourself. Here are a few hair-healthy recipes that can help you achieve great hair!

Milk & Honey Hair Smoothie

- 1 can of pure coconut milk *(rich moisturizer—hydrates, conditions and de-frizzes hair)*
- 1 ripe avocado *(natural source of protein—chemical processes rob the hair of protein)*
- 2 tablespoons of pure honey *(conditions and adds sheen)*

- 2 tablespoons of olive oil *(fatty oil that moisturizes and conditions dry hair)*

Directions:

Add ingredients to blender. Mix at high speed until your concoction reaches a smoothie consistency.

Store in refrigerator for up to two weeks. You can warm up your hair smoothie in the microwave before next application... just enough to de-chill.

Substitutions:

- Feel free to substitute the olive oil for any natural oil of your choice.
- Add an additional tablespoon of olive oil for extra dry hair.
- Add two additional tablespoons o honey for hair that needs more sheen.

Instructions for Use:

- Section hair into four segments.

- Generously apply evenly to hair, from root to ends concentrating on ends...as they are the most prone to damage.
- Smooth hair into a protective style (e.g. braided ponytail, or bun).
- Enjoy your day at the pool, lake, or ocean!

Coconut and Shea Butter Treatment Mask
Ingredients:

- 4oz unrefined shea butter
- 5 tablespoons of coconut oil
- 2 tablespoons of olive oil
- 3 tablespoons of pomegranate seed oil
- 10 drops of red raspberry seed oil

Directions:

Bring three cups of water to boil. Set aside. Seal the shea butter in a small Tupperware bowl and place on top of the water for three minutes. DO NOT DIRECTLY HEAT THE BUTTER or the butter will become granulated. Combine all ingredients in a large mixing bowl. Mix on medium speed, with a hand mixer for three to five minutes or until the butter starts to form a whipped texture. For easy use, scoop your Shea Butter and Raspberry Repair Mask into a Ziploc bag, and cut the tip to dispense. Shampoo as usual, rinse well. Apply Coconut and Shea Butter Treatment Mask

Benefits

Shea Butter—Absorbs into the scalp and hair and restores over processed hair as a result of blow drying, perms, relaxers or dyes. Protects hair from the sun (heat) and from the harshness of cold weather (lack of moisture).

Coconut Oil— a natural protein reconstructor. It's ability to bind to the natural protein structure of the hair makes it an excellent oil of choice for damaged, dry, African American hair. It helps the hair retain its natural moisture content and reinforces the hair fiber, making it stronger.

Olive Oil—Loaded with antioxidants, this powerhouse oil increases blood flow that stimulate the follicles, which then produce thicker strands. Also great for dry, itchy scalp and dandruff relief.

Pomegranate Seed oil—The high antioxidant and vitamin content of this natural moisturizer help to increase the blood circulation in the scalp, strengthen blood vessels and thereby promote healthy hair growth. It also helps reduce flakiness, itchiness of the scalp, common in dry hair.

Red raspberry seed oil—heals, strengthens and moisturizes dry hair and scalp. Adds elasticity and suppleness, while providing immediate sparkle and shine

Guava & Honey Hair Mask
Ingredients:

1 ripe guava
2 teaspoons of honey

3 drops of lemon essential oil

½ cup of organic coconut oil.

Directions

Peel and remove the seeds out of the guava. Blend the fruit and coconut oil at low speed for 30 seconds. Add the honey and lemon oil, blend on medium speed until the honey is mixed well into the fruit. Shampoo hair, blot out excess water and apply hair mask. Leave the Guava and Honey Hair Mask on for 15 minutes. Rinse with warm water and condition as usual. Shiny, soft, moisturized tresses await you!

Benefits:

Guava- A powerhouse of nutrients including Vitamin A, vitamin C, folic acid, potassium, copper, and other phytochemicals beneficial for healthy hair growth.

Honey—excellent humectant, softens the cuticle and prevents hair loss by preventing loss of moisture.

Lemon essential oil—The best essential oil for dry, curly hair. It stimulates the sebaceous glands to produce oil, which is key for healthy, shiny, strong hair.

Coconut oil—Conditions the hair shaft and increases shine and the hair fiber's pliability. Excellent sealant that locks in moisture

Roses & Jojoba Oil Hair Therapy

Ingredients:

½ cup of rose water

3 tablespoons of jojoba oil

1 tablespoons of vitamin e oil.

Directions:

Heat the rose water on the stove until it is warm but not too hot to touch. This will help the rose water and oils blend together. Stir in the jojoba oil. If it does not completely blend, that is okay. Pour the mixture into the blender. If it has become hot enough to create steam, let the mixture cool slightly before you pour it. Add the vitamin E oil, if your hair is severely damaged. Blend the mixture on high for two minutes. This should cause the ingredients to blend completely. The result will be a clear or nearly clear liquid. Store the conditioner in a plastic shampoo bottle. You can use it up to four times a week to repair hair. Work the conditioner into your hair from root to tip, and let it sit on your hair for at least ten minutes before rinsing with lukewarm water.

Banana & Avocado Hair Mask

Ingredients:

- 1 medium banana
- 1/2 avocado
- 1 egg yolk
- 3 tablespoons buttermilk
- 3 tablespoons extra virgin olive oil

Directions:

Mash banana, egg and avocado in a small bowl. Add remaining ingredients and stir until well combined. Apply to hair from roots to tips. Leave in for 30 minutes and then wash out with a moisturizing shampoo. Double the recipe for long hair.

Benefits:

> **Banana**—rich in natural oils and vitamins that help to soften and protect the hair.. Creates manageability, shine, growth and controls dandruff.
>
> **Avocado**— Rich in fatty acids that are a real must for dry brittle hair. Creates soft and shiny tresses.
>
> **Egg**—rich in protein needed to smooth the hair shaft, increase resistance to breakage by strengthening strands and reduce split ends. .
>
> **Buttermilk**—natural fatty milk that moisturizes hair.

Champagne Toast

Ingredients:

- ½ cup of champagne (I prefer organic champagne—my favorite Champagne Prestige Millesime 1997)

- ½ cup of warm distilled water

- OPTIONAL—for those that suffer from dry scalp, massage jojoba oil into the scalp before shampooing.

Directions:

Mix champagne with distilled water. For easy pouring, I recommend putting the champagne mixture back in the bottle before heading to the shower. Shampoo and condition hair as usual. Rinse well. Pour the Champagne mixture throughout hair. DO NOT RINSE. You can do this rinse up to three times for really dull, porous hair.

All of these recipes are a decadent treat for your tresses and a great way to use products you may have at home. Ultimately, it's all for the same goal—making your hair healthy and fab!

CPSIA information can be obtained at www.ICGtesting.com
Printed in the USA
LVOW06s0325050215

425794LV00025B/788/P